THE CHICAGO PUBLIC LIBRARY

FORM 19   AUG -- 1997

LOVING MADLY, LOVING SANELY

How to Keep Your Brain from Ruining Your Love Life

Andrew Abarbanel, M.D.

KENSINGTON BOOKS
http://www.kensingtonbooks.com

KENSINGTON BOOKS are published by

Kensington Publishing Corp.
850 Third Avenue
New York, NY 10022

Copyright © 1997 by Andrew Abarbanel

All rights reserved. No part of this book may be reproduced in any form or by any means without the prior written consent of the Publisher, excepting brief quotes used in reviews.

Kensington and the K logo Reg. U.S. Pat. & TM Off.

Library of Congress Card Catalog Number: 96-079080
ISBN 1-57566-161-6

First Printing: May, 1997
10   9   8   7   6   5   4   3   2   1

Printed in the United States of America

To Katie

Al miglior capolavoro

ACKNOWLEDGMENTS

Not surprisingly, my friends, family, colleagues, teachers, and patients have taught me everything I've put in this book—intentionally or otherwise. My patients, especially, taught me more than I could have imagined, including how badly this book needed to be written. Almost without exception, their struggles and their triumphs moved me deeply. My friends Tom Broadbent and Peter Wyden persevered in their belief that a writer lurked within me, long before I admitted to them (or to me) that I agreed. Buzz and Chris Armanini; Phil Berger; John Peterson; Rennie and Kyle Miller; Barrie O'Brien; Pat Baker; Kathy Major; Eugene Hyman; Leah Cheli; Nic Smith; Miriam, Art, and Doug Bodin; and Anne and Steve Cone helped keep my spirits inflated in those times when reality's juggernaut demoralized me or when my talent or enthusiasm ran out on their own. Molly Friedrich, Sheri Holman, Paul Cirone, and Frances Jalet-Miller at the Aaron M. Priest Agency, and Sarah Gallick and Tracy Bernstein at Kensington all delighted me with literary wisdom and insight and, like Tom and Peter, touched me with their emotional generosity. Michèle Eisenberg added the lovely touch of linking my daughter Katie to Dante Alighieri.

If, as he said, Newton stood on the shoulders of giants in producing his work, I rode on those of angels in writing this book. Katie, David, Daniel, Rachel—know always that this book, as everything I've done since April 27, 1986, has been driven by a single engine: the wish to make the world a better place for your future. And, Donna—know that you've given me the finest days and years I've known. You were always on my mind as I wrote this book, however preoccupied I may have seemed.

CONTENTS

Introduction: Mind, Brain, and Love Life	*1*
1. The Anatomy of Interpersonal Distress	*15*
2. Attention Deficit Disorder and Interpersonal Relationships	*33*
3. Mood Disorders and Their Effect on Relationships	*57*
4. Anxiety Disorders and Their Effect on Relationships	*85*
5. How Your Brain Can Get You into the Wrong Relationship	*99*
6. How Your Brain Can Ruin a Good Relationship	*119*
7. How Your Brain Can Keep You Out of Relationships Altogether	*137*
8. Popular Misconceptions: Why People Won't Swallow Even the Idea of Medication	*159*
9. What's a Couple to Do?	*179*
10. How to Use a Psychiatrist	*197*
11. Potential Problems and Pitfalls	*213*
Epilogue	*221*

LOVING MADLY, LOVING SANELY

INTRODUCTION: MIND, BRAIN, AND LOVE LIFE

Dawn Patrol

Introducing a book is a lot like making love for the first time—you have an idea of what you're trying to get across, but how to present it, and do it, and how it might be received, worry you. Fortunately, in this case I had some timely help from a young woman whose story perfectly illustrates what I want to tell you. I'd fallen asleep one night, puzzling about how to preface the book—and was awoken at five A.M. by a phone call from a frantic woman I didn't know. Her name was Dawn and she had to talk to me *right now*. She was being evicted that morning by a villainous landlord, her boyfriend had left her and wouldn't help her move, her mother hasn't spoken to her since the last time this happened, and her father hadn't had anything to do with her for years. She was crying throughout her lament, but there was a tinge of irritability in her voice that warned me I'd better respond very sympathetically and very helpfully or I'd be the next entry on the list of villains I was hearing about.

But it was five A.M., and I was still only half awake. I did my best to sort out her story, but she interrupted to tell me that she needed to see me soon. Had to—eight A.M., at the latest.

Eight A.M.?

I was clearly not toeing the line very well—she heard some reluctance in my voice, and this pushed her on to a second round of lament. No one listened. Not her parents, certainly—they just wanted her to cheer up, get organized, and get on with her life. Her girlfriends wouldn't listen—they say she gets so tediously self-absorbed when she's down and even more scatterbrained than usual, and— She couldn't go on from there, but cried for a long time, stopping only here and there to mention someone else who wouldn't listen, or had run off on her, lied to her, or otherwise let her down. The theme of being treated badly was so pronounced in what she told me (when I thought about the call later that day, I could recall at least thirteen villains) that after making sure she wasn't suicidal and setting up an appointment (at ten A.M.), I told her that there was something I wanted her to think about until then:

Is there something you do to bring out the worst in people?

This, of course, being the last thing any person wants to think about—especially alone in the dead of night—it sent her off the phone and right to sleep so that she didn't have to. I'd hoped it would.

The events and changes in Dawn's life—especially in her love life—starting with the five A.M. ambush, are what this book is about. It's for anyone who wants to improve his or her chances for better and longer-lasting relationships—whether you are as unhappy as Dawn was that morning, or simply stymied by milder issues in yourself (or in anyone or everyone else). Dawn, as I said, presents an unusually clear example of many of the factors we'll need to consider. Back to her story, then.

Over the next several weeks I learned that under an insatiable neediness and inability to wait even a moment for anything she felt she needed, and a terrible drivenness to get whatever that happened to be, she was terribly depressed. And, along with her depression, which ebbed and flowed over time, there was a continual restlessness and scatter to her thinking and activity. It was very difficult for her to sit still, keep to a single task or topic of conversation, or listen to anyone for more than a few moments without wandering off to something completely unrelated. She was the prototypic flake who rarely followed up on promises, finished anything she started, or sat still long enough to get anything right, relationships included.

There was a great deal about her, in other words, that brought out the worst in people. Her gloominess and inconsolability got people around her down in the dumps or, to protect themselves from this, upset with her for not cheering up. Once or twice a year there would be weeks or months in which she'd lose interest in everything, cry continuously, and stay in bed for days. Some days during these episodes, though, she'd be irritable to the point of cantankerous, blaming anyone and everyone for what was wrong with her life. Even in the best of times, though, she'd depress people with her unshakable gloominess, or else drive them to distraction with her scatterbrained neglect of promises and her forgetting, misplacing, or otherwise mismanaging work assignments, social plans, and any other responsibility that came her way.

The most poignant thing I learned over those few weeks, and the most important feature of her story for this book, was this: Despite her clingy depressiveness, fussy irritability, and near-chaotic mental process, under it all was a very nice and very attractive person who loved her family and friends. Her social and family life were strained and her love life was nonexistent only because of her moodiness and scatteredness. To put it plainly, her interpersonal life was being undone because she had two of the most common psychological disorders: depression and an attention disorder.

When I gave her medication for those disorders and watched them come under control in two or three weeks, there emerged a calmer, more organized, and much more personable Dawn that had been overshadowed by the symptoms of these disorders nearly all her life. Over the next few months her relationships with family and friends improved remarkably—and, Dawn being a very attractive young woman, several men who had earlier fled now became very interested in her.

It's wonderful to participate in something like this with dozens of Dawns each year—it makes the five A.M. phone calls and even the boredom of medical school and internship seem like a small price to have paid. And for the Dawns themselves, the gratification is much greater—it's a rebirth, or sometimes even a first birth, into an interpersonal world that's been out of reach for years, if not from the start.

But nothing this rewarding comes easy—despite the fact that efforts like these are so often so successful, they're nonetheless becoming very controversial. The human spirit, some say, is being neglected by people like me. You can't treat the spiritual or existential needs of people like Dawn with pills, they say, or I'm crushing my patients' chances to deal with the real underlying psychological issues. Others contend that any mind-altering substance is by its very nature a bad thing, akin to an addiction, and must be avoided. These are serious charges, and deserve serious answers.

Throughout the book, then, I'll address as respectfully and carefully as I can the criticism of the ideas and types of treatment people like me are finding so useful for people like Dawn. I can't help wishing, though, that I didn't have to, but instead could invite the critics and skeptics to sit in with me and see Dawn firsthand during the initial three or four weeks of treatment. Or have them watch Dawn's mother when she saw her daughter for the first time after treatment. Until that moment she had never seen her little girl, whether at five or twenty-five, able to sit still for two minutes, to not cry or run away or lash out at the gentlest of constructive criticism, or to listen to what was said to her and hear it—all of it. Up to that moment, Dawn had heard only the bits and pieces that her attention disorder had let in and that her depression had shaped into whatever abuse it cared to, but now she heard all of it, love and caring, criticism and praise, pronouns and conjunctions (Dawn's mother is an English teacher). She was feeling all the things I felt at the birth of our first child, when the obstetrician persevered through some tense moments to hand me our baby, unharmed by the intricacies and mysteries of childbirth, and as lovely as the aurora—I was too choked with emotion to express myself with anything but tears of joy.

I wish, too, that the critics and skeptics could listen in as Dawn herself came to realize—as people treated for depression or attention disorders almost invariably realize after a few weeks or months of psychiatric treatment—that she wasn't a gangly, clumsy, unattractive, and unintelligent twenty-five-year-old teenager. Rather, she was a bright and lovely twenty-five-year-old woman with a future, a future into which a loving partner and children, if desired, would fit as comfortably as a key in a lock.

Of course, I can't have every skeptic sit in on my sessions and personally witness success stories like Dawn's. But I can urge people to read them here. The book is based on two decades of treating people like Dawn or couples in which one or the other (or both) partners was as troubled as she was, and watching their suffering greatly diminish, or dissipate altogether, as the tools of the trade came to the rescue. I've written, then, about the plight of the millions of men or women with treatable psychological problems that invariably distress and routinely undo their relationships or their chances for relationships—to tell you that it doesn't have to be this way.

What follows, however, isn't for or about only those people with serious psychiatric problems. We all have something of the conditions psychiatrists list in diagnostic manuals—if only to a mild degree. We all get depressed—for a while—if something bad enough happens, and we all get scattered or obsessive—to some degree—if enough bad things happen all at once. We'll see throughout the book that even the mildest cases of psychiatric problems upset relationships in almost the same ways that more serious cases do—and that they have the same biological basis and respond to the same treatment. Sometimes, in fact, the milder cases cause more trouble because they're harder to identify, but can undo relationships just as completely.

This book, then, is for anyone interested in having a good love relationship, whether this means holding on to one that's already good, avoiding one that's guaranteed to be bad, or losing whatever inhibitions and fears are keeping relationships out of your reach. Unless I state the contrary, what I've said applies equally to men and women, men and men or women and women. And though I'll leave the fact aside to focus on love relations, it often applies to relationships of all kinds, including work relations, friendships, student-teacher relations, and so on.

There are a million things that ruin people's chances for good love relationships. Only one sector of these is examined here—the group of disorders like the ones that caused so much trouble for Dawn. The good news is that these conditions are treatable in almost all cases, and that treating someone for them is so helpful to his or her relationships. It's not such good news, on the other hand, that the more than fifty years of successful treatment of people like Dawn are denied or dismissed by a great many people who, unlike the more serious critics I mentioned a moment ago, often know almost nothing—if not absolutely nothing—about the conditions and treatments they're devaluing.

Hence this introduction to the common treatable psychological disorders that menace so many relationships. Most of us can see them every day if we look around, and learn how perniciously they can unravel even the best relationships—or put them out of reach in the first place.

The Dawn of a New Approach

The first stirrings of this book grew to maturity, so to speak, along with my own maturation as a psychiatrist. My psychiatric training began at Harvard's McLean Hospital in the seventies. McLean is a sprawling three-hundred-acre bastion of psychiatry founded in 1811 when its first patient was treated for demonic possession—by whipping. It's progressed a bit since then as a number of more enlightened schools of thought about psychiatric treatment have flourished, though not often cooperated, there. The school of old-guard psychoanalysis was dominant in the decades around the middle of the century, and applied Freudian ideas and techniques to treat the symptoms of the major psychiatric disorders—schizophrenia, depression, mania, and the major anxiety and attentional disorders, conditions I'll describe later in the book. Currently, the school of biological psychiatry, which studies the biological and biochemical aspects of mental illness, is in ascension. This group develops and administers medication and other biologically based treatments to control the symptoms of the major psychiatric disorders. There was also a department of social work, which taught the importance of family therapy and imposed it on patients' families. Finally, there was a small department of behaviorists, who developed and practiced techniques of behavior modification.

Being part of Harvard, McLean had attracted the superstars of these subfields to its faculty. And being part of Harvard, the members of each subfield knew that they were the elite—the one tried-and-true psychiatric denomination among the scores on the market. The psychoanalysts, for example, looked down on the biological psychiatrists as psychologically unsophisticated, and therefore unaware that the essence of psychological distress resides in the set of psychological theories that Freud set forth around a hundred years ago. The biological psychiatrists, in turn, looked down on the analysts as outmoded—the action, they knew, was in biochemical and brain mechanisms. Neither the psychoanalysts nor the biologists took much stock of the behaviorists or social workers, but if they had, they would have looked down on them as upstarts—sadly unschooled in the intricacies of psychological theory or science. The behaviorists in their turn looked down on the first two groups, as did the social workers—each group knowing that behaviorism or family dynamics was where the real action was. The subgroups ambushed the patients sequentially, and then assaulted each other simultaneously, each demanding the trophy when a patient endured the onslaught and got better in spite of it. It was tribal warfare at its highest intensity, the stuff anthropologists dream of.

For those of us in training, on the other hand, it was less a dream than a nightmare, as we tried for three or four years to integrate each of these uniquely correct and mutually contradictory approaches to mental illness. I chose my tribe early—the psychoanalysts—and did what I could to tolerate and placate the others enough to get through. Then I escaped from McLean altogether to practice psychiatry in more laid-back California, where I'd gone to medical school. Once there, I spent some time doing further training in psychoanalysis, which consists of several years of seminars and supervised cases (that you do in whatever time you can steal away from your practice and family), after which you are a certified expert on the agonies and intricacies of depth psychology, Freudian style, i.e., patients lying on a couch four or five days a week for six or eight or ten years.

Meanwhile, in my practice (my day job, so to speak), my patients and colleagues were introducing me to a whole new world of psychiatry that Freud hadn't known about—largely because he'd died in 1939. I began to study the biology of mental illness and the use of medications in greater earnest than I had at McLean; I found that I could treat patients with both medication and talking therapy, and that the whole was greater than the sum of the parts—that is, the patients improved more quickly and in a more profound way than with purely talking therapy, and the psychiatric symptoms (like depression or anxiety) improved sooner and more completely than with medication alone.

That was when the book began in earnest (though I didn't know it yet). The locals always send the new guy in town the most difficult cases (it's a rite of tribal initiation—like internship or circumcision). Patients came who were too depressed to talk, and just sat and didn't get better. Or they talked about their problems and I talked about their problems, but they didn't get better. Sometimes they got worse. It was the same with the other major psychiatric problems, like eating disorders and phobias. But when I started using medications along with talking therapy with these patients, it helped a great deal. They became much less depressed or psychotic or bulimic, and were able to deal with their psychological issues much more effectively. It wasn't, as at McLean, a matter of whether I thought about a patient biologically or psychologically. It became a question of how well I could combine the approaches—and it seemed to work pretty well.

Political realities can teach you something too. With the deification of the bottom line escalating throughout the eighties and nineties, cost effectiveness began to determine how insurance and managed-care companies delivered mental health coverage. Thus they sent people with psychological problems to counselors who are less expensive than psychiatrists. Psychiatrists were reserved for limited consultations and second opinions. The effect on my practice has been an increase in the number of patients I see in consultation—generally to determine if medication or other medically based treatment is likely to help them.

For many of these patients I do recommend medication and then see them periodically in follow-up. You see a great many people this way—for me it's been at least three hundred over the last few years, a large enough number to let me spot trends and patterns and test my ideas about them. Many of the patients are referred by marriage counselors; for the majority, the psychiatric disorder improves with treatment, and a significant percentage stop marriage counseling. They find that once one or the other (or both) partners are no longer depressed or obsessed or phobic, the marriage works much better, and they don't need counseling. Wives, for example, who'd complained that their husbands were too lazy or irresponsible to help support the family learned that in reality their husbands had been depressed, preoccupied with phobias, impaired by attentional disorders, or the like. Once the disorder was treated, the husbands went back to work and the marriage most often went back to normal. At other times we found that people who had been incorrigibly promiscuous were doing this only during the manic swings of undiagnosed manic-depressive disorders. Appropriate treatment cleaned up this problem too. The same sort of thing happened with all the common disorders. It was as if I were doing marriage counseling completely by accident—and doing it pretty well considering that I almost never saw the partners together.

Some patients do need to continue counseling. Sometimes, for example, the effect of the psychiatric disorder has caused so much damage to the relationship that the couple needs ongoing psychological work. At other times the disorder has distorted a patient's personality so much that he needs ongoing counseling to learn (or relearn) the skills and attitudes necessary to be in a good relationship. Fortunately, each of these endeavors goes much better (and quicker) because of the medication or other psychiatric treatment.

There were some disorders that I could help in this way more than others, and some not at all. I'll concentrate on the ones that most commonly disrupt relationships and that respond best to psychiatric treatment. The syndromes, discussed in detail in Chapters Two through Four, are depression and mania and their minor variants, attention deficit disorder, obsessive-compulsive disorder, phobias, and other major anxiety disorders. The last fifty years of research on the brain and its mechanisms have produced a mountain of evidence that these disorders have a major biological basis. This work has led to medication and other treatments that in most cases can control the symptoms of these disorders. Paradoxically enough, these are usually much easier to treat than many less severe conditions. The situation is a lot like the one my father used to joke about. He was an old-time general practitioner, and liked to tell a patient with a cough or the sniffles that he couldn't cure the cold, but if he'd have a little patience and let it blossom into pneumonia, *that* he could cure. Of course, we can and do treat the relatively less catastrophic syndromes like crises of identity or gender confusion, but since medications or other purely medical approaches don't affect them, it can take years of talking therapy to mitigate the difficulties.

I should emphasize that when I use the term "medically based treatment," it's as a shorthand for a group of treatments for the biological component of psychiatric conditions. I may from time to time give the impression that the only biological treatment modality is the use of medication—that is not the case (although the majority of these treatments do include the use of psychotropic medications). As the last two chapters will suggest, it's probably accurate to include behavior modification and cognitive therapy among the biological treatments—and absolutely to include the new techniques of neurofeedback.

I'm aware that not everyone accepts the idea that the major disorders have a biological basis. But I do not believe there is any question about it—even without the past half century of research and clinical experience. The reason is this: Each day I see that despite tremendous differences in personality, intelligence, lifestyle, and culture, the same symptom clusters appear in every person with the same disorder. With a depressive episode, for example, each patient presents a cluster of complaints from the same list: low mood, lack of interest in life, trouble concentrating, disturbed sleep and appetite, hopelessness about the future, and so on. And the same group of medications (or other biologically based treatments) corrects only those symptoms and leaves the rest of the personality alone. Anything that stereotypic for so many people has to be determined biologically—it's inconceivable to me that the random forces of personal experience could produce such results in such large groups of people. Psychological conditions without a biological basis, on the other hand, vary tremendously in their symptoms and in what helps resolve them. Problems in this group, like identity crises, difficulties with authority, problems with parenting, or vocational confusion (to list the last four examples I've seen this week) are as different as the people who struggle with them. What it takes to unravel them also varies—from doing nothing whatever to doing ten years of psychoanalysis.

What This Book Is (and Isn't) About

I've belabored these details because they're what brought me to the message of the book—that the biologically based disorders

I've mentioned do a great deal of damage to relationships and that treating them can go a long way toward repairing the damage, often in short order. Dawn's experience with depression and attention deficit disorder is an absolutely typical example. It's a great shame that so few people know about these conditions, or know how common they are and how often they disrupt or downright demolish relationships. Ignorance of what a partner is going through, for example, leads too many otherwise sane and well-intentioned people to further demoralize their depressed partners with inane demands to "cheer up," or drive to further distraction their ADD partners with equally exasperating advice like "just get organized." People need to learn that these disorders are not the result of laziness or bad attitude or stupidity, but rather are bona fide medical disorders that no act of will, no matter how monumental, will budge a single millimeter. Both partners need to understand that the conditions can be treated effectively, often in a matter of weeks, and that very often the relationship returns to normal or becomes normal for the first time. By understanding these things, people locked in bad relationships, or locked out of good ones, stand a much better chance to fix, or find, a stable and satisfying relationship.

One of the themes that organized this book is that each disorder typically leads to one or more of the things that damage or doom relationships—infidelity, abuse, neglect, personal or career failure and its consequences, or serious difficulty in communication. The driven hypersexuality, overactivity, and distractibility of mania and hypomania, for example, often lead to infidelity. The impulsive distractibility and exaggerated tendency to boredom (with the resulting fickleness) of the attention disorders often lead to career failure, neglect of one's partner, and infidelity. The low energy and self-esteem, inability to concentrate, irritability, and other symptoms of depression lead to career failure, neglect, verbal and physical abuse, or infidelity—and so on down our list of disorders.

The effect on communication is especially disruptive. Human communication, it seems to me, is implausible in the best of circumstances. People are wildly different in their psychological issues, quirks, and hang-ups, in their benign or traumatic experiences growing up, in their personality styles, intellectual styles, cultural backgrounds, interests, talents, preferences, and on and on. Given all this, it's remarkable that any two of us can communicate at all, let alone for an extended period of time while continuing to like each other. Mix in a psychiatric disorder in one or both partners, and the fact that communication sometimes persists is so miraculous that it's major evidence for the existence of a benign God—in my opinion. Even Freud, a deity himself in some circles, thought that without the bond of sexual attraction, men and women would have long since exterminated one another.

All things considered (except the details of procreation), communication probably does more to prevent extinction than sexuality. It does this by allowing partners to teach each other how to get along—both by avoiding the things that make trouble, and by doing the things that help the relationship. Good communication gives a relationship a set of checks and balances that keep the frailties and iniquities of human nature from derailing it. Anything that impairs your ability to communicate with your partner impairs this regulation—and nothing impairs communication like a psychiatric disorder.

For the formal organization of this book itself, I've kept the focus on relationships, and on how the psychiatric disorders (including their milder forms present in so many of us) affect relationships. The initial chapters are devoted to the attentional, mood, and anxiety disorders, with an emphasis on their interpersonal aspects. The middle chapters explain and give examples of how these disorders can get people into the wrong relationships, tumble them out of good ones, or keep them out of relationships altogether. The final chapters suggest how to help your relationship survive one (or more) of these disorders, whether it ambushes you in the middle of a good relationship or is present from the start.

There are several things this book is not about. I'll state them explicitly because I worry that people may take issue with things I never intended to say but that they may be accustomed to hearing from people like me. First, I'm not going to describe a group of white-coated automata who, instead of listening to their patients, give them magical "happy pills" that drown out their worries by dulling their minds, along with their sentience and dignity—all in a pink cloud of joyful mindlessness. This is not what psychiatrists are or what their medications do. When treatment works properly, a patient has no sense of being drugged or altered, except that his painful symptoms are gone or at least substantially diminished. As I will show, with appropriate medication a person can deal with his problems better because his thinking is clearer and his emotional posture is stronger, and he is therefore better able to deal with whatever may be rocking his boat. Put another way, the medication does not make a person euphoric, or even happy all the time, rather, it returns (or brings) him to normal, without excessive pain or exhilaration at the ordinary ups and downs of everyday life.

Second, the book does not discount psychology, spirituality, or any other human virtue. It's foolish, for example, to think that because a person's symptoms can be alleviated with medication that no attention should be paid to his interpersonal anxieties, fears about sexuality, struggles with authority, and so on. As I've said, treatment with medication makes talking therapy work better in dealing with issues like these. On the other hand, not treating a biologically based disorder can trap both the patient and the therapist in a morass of jargonizing and agonizing that goes on forever but doesn't solve any problems. In the same vein, attention to the status of a person's biochemistry doesn't mean ignoring the status of his spirituality. My experience of treating psychiatric disorders in a number of clergymen has been that their faith in God and man is enriched, not diminished, with treatment.

Third, this book is not against couples therapy. Quite the contrary—one of its goals is to make relationships work better. Nor does it argue that all couples therapy must be augmented by medication. As I said, the effects of treatable psychological disorders represent only one sector of the million problems that plague interpersonal relations. But it is a very important and very common problem, and if a partner has a treatable psychiatric disorder, it should be treated.

The ideas in this book are illustrated by a number of clinical cases; these were inspired by real people but the details have been laundered, divvied up, reassembled, and disguised enough that if you recognize yourself or someone else in this book, you can be absolutely certain that it is not you or anyone you know. Thus George Balusteri of Chapter One, all appearances aside, is not my father-in-law or yours. On the other hand, if you do think you find yourself here, your misperception may be telling you something, and you should therefore take whatever passage you're reading all the more seriously.

Speaking of Mr. B., I invariably find that when I read a book like this, the various Janes and Joans and Jonathans get so mixed up in my head that I can never keep them or the details of their problems straight. Because of this, I've used names like Balusteri, Satterly, or Worley to approximate the blustery, scattered, or whirling characteristics that define these people and make them useful for us. Also, throughout the book I use the old-fashioned "he" and "him" to stand for both genders, solely to avoid awkwardness and repetition.

The tone of this book is occasionally playful. Be assured that this implies no disrespect for the sobering and sometimes tragic nature of the problems I discuss. Mark Twain said that the secret source of humor is sadness, not joy. The depth of suffering one confronts in dealing with the topics of this book can be profound, and has dragged many a therapist down into despair along with his patients. I've softened the presentation with humor and anecdote to avoid draining my reader of his energy and enthusiasm, and therefore of his capacity to understand and enjoy the book and what it says.

All that settled, we move to the thorny problems the book takes on, and begin with the case of the blustery George Balusteri.

CHAPTER 1

THE ANATOMY OF INTERPERSONAL DISTRESS

"Go get your head examined!"—Mrs. Balusteri

The first time Jennine Balusteri came to my office, she couldn't stop crying. She was so upset, in fact, that it wasn't until the end of the hour that I had any idea why. Jennine, now sixty years old, had been married for forty of them, she told me, but the marriage had been a nightmare almost from the start. George had been charming and solicitous during their courtship, and although he'd been a bit gloomy and impatient whenever they couldn't be together, she was shocked by what was to emerge after they'd married: a controlling, demanding, abusive grump of a man who was no longer charming or solicitous to anyone, especially not to his wife. Each day began with a tirade about her inadequacy and the misery it caused him, and only as the day wore on and apparently wore him down would Mr. Balusteri relent and show even a hint of the gentle and loving man he'd once been. By then, however, his wife was too hurt, frightened, and angry to enjoy or encourage this softening of his mood.

I asked why she'd stayed with him all those years. She loved him, she told me, and you don't leave a man just because he gets a little grumpy. Had she looked for help before now? Yes, she had. She'd talked with her girlfriends; but after withstanding four decades of their advice, she'd learned that however well intentioned, it all boiled down to whatever each woman imagined that she herself would have done if she were in this marriage and if she were the woman she imagined herself to be. Leave him, don't leave him, they said, have an affair, don't have an affair, put your foot down more, don't put your foot down so much—all the things they wished they could be doing, or not doing, in their own marriages.

She'd also read relationship books. She read about women who loved too much and the men who abused them for this, about women who hated too much and the men who loved them for this, about women who are addicted to men and about the men who dance away from this. She read about smart women and stupid women and suffering women and love-addicted women—all, somehow, miserable without their men and miserable with their men. She read about the psychology and the transactionality and the spirituality of relationships, and then about the mythology and even the planetary astronomy of relationships. And despite the fact that each book seemed to dispute all the others, she found much of herself in each of them, but also found that whenever she tried to apply what they'd told her, it failed miserably. Neither she nor her husband nor their relationship improved.

Then she went to the workshops. She learned how to be more of a feminist, then less of a feminist, more sexual and then less sexual, more adult, more childlike, more demanding, more compliant, and so on through all the steps, stages, enneagrams, and other ways to adjust yourself and your lifestyle to the ideals of countless authors and organizations—and found the same tantalizing enlightenment and utter inapplicability that she had with the books. Finally, after forty years of suffering from George's bluster and abuse, and from the advice, books, and seminars, she gave up on authority great and small, followed her heart, and walked out on her husband. She told him she was leaving because he was impossible and she was miserable and that if he expected to see her again, he should get his head examined.

She hadn't meant that literally, of course. She meant it angrily and rhetorically, as a way to tell him that this was absolutely the end of the marriage. Her husband, however, stunned by her leaving, heard it literally—as a prerequisite for reconciling with her—and did go get his head examined. He saw a psychiatrist, that is, and was diagnosed as suffering from a chronic depressive disorder. The doctor prescribed Prozac, and in a matter of a few days Mr. Balusteri had a remarkable response. His sullen moods and gloomy outlook, his explosive irritability and tyrannical intimidation of everyone around him, resolved almost immediately. Two weeks into their separation, he telephoned his wife and told her of the transformation. Despite her skepticism, she recognized in his voice something of the change he'd announced. Once again tossing her customary timidity to the winds, she came to see him. To her astonishment, she found that what he'd said was true: Here was a gentle and accommodating sixty-five-year-old man looking and acting more like Pinocchio's gentle Geppetto than the Vesuvian Svengali of the previous forty years. Now it was her turn to be stunned. She moved back in that very day, and her husband had been a perfect gentleman ever since.

So why was she still crying?

In her exhilaration about finally, after forty years, freeing herself from Mr. B., she'd gone completely against her nature and begun a love affair with a man that she'd admired (though never until then desired) for years. But now that George was once again the man she'd fallen in love with forty years earlier, she felt terribly guilty about her infidelity. Since George was so understanding about her malfeasance, one might think that Mrs. B. would get past her guilt rather easily—but she couldn't. The product of a strict religious upbringing, all her life she had become outlandishly guilty over the slightest transgression of any rule, civil or ecclesiastical. To make things worse, her husband's critical demeanor throughout the marriage had had the paradoxical effect of softening her guilt over anything she'd done wrong. This was because she was able to struggle so vigorously against his criticism of her that she'd distract herself from her criticism of herself. Now that he was so forgiving, she couldn't do this— and fury from the inside being much harder to hold off than fury from the outside, her guilty conscience was crushing her. The pressure of the unrelenting guilt soon pushed her to the edge of a suicidally intense depression. Only the fact that to Mrs. B. suicide would be a greater sin than adultery kept her alive. It was nonetheless a worrisome circumstance, and when she asked me to prescribe an antidepressant for her, I complied.

Like Mr. B., Mrs. B. had a good response to medication, though hers was a little more gradual. Within a month or so, both were doing and feeling very well indeed. Mr. B. remained his old self, and Mrs. B. could now forgive herself for her transgressions and therefore enjoy the change in her husband. Now, she assured me, they were past the years of misery and could get on to the important issues of married life in one's sixties: reminiscing about old times and exulting about young grandchildren.

It's wonderful to observe, let alone participate in, a process like this. A man, after forty years of chronic gloominess, irritability, and blustery harassment of his wife, becomes gentle and considerate. A woman, after forty years, sets aside her lifelong timidity and guiltiness, learns to ask for what she wants from her husband, and gets it. A relationship becomes loving, reciprocal, and comfortable after four decades of dissatisfaction and despair. Understand—I've chosen an especially striking example to illustrate my themes. Most couples do need ongoing counseling and sometimes in-depth individual work to stabilize the improvements and undo what the psychiatric disorders involved have done to both the individual and his relationships. But those couples work much more effectively in psychological treatment after psychiatric treatment. And there are many couples like (or almost like) the Balusteris, who, once treated psychiatrically, do very well almost entirely on their own. In only a few weeks time, and with no talking therapy, no seminars, and almost no counseling, the Balusteris improved remarkably. Most of the psychological adjustments were done on their own. As I said, it's wonderful to see this. It isn't so wonderful, on the other hand, to know that millions of men and women like Jennine and George (I'll estimate just how many in a moment) suffer through miserable relationships and have no idea whatever of the factors generating their misery.

Why is this? That stories like that of the Balusteris are played out every day in the offices of thousands of psychiatrists is not a hypothesis—it's a fact. I've watched it, and my colleagues have watched it, over and over. Sometimes, of course, individual or couples therapy is needed to get the couple on track, but, as I've said, this treatment is much more efficient than it is without medication or other biologically based treatment. All the books about men and women, smart or stupid, from Mars or Venus or Pluto, belabor every detail and combination of details of the psychological issues between people, but they leave out the indispensable fact that a great deal of the misery between people is grounded in their biology.

It must not be ignored that both the man who abuses his wife and the wife who is afraid to leave—each of whose personality is discussed, dissected, and digested in a thousand books—are very likely depressed, and that their depression is what motivates the abusive or masochistic behavior. Or that a man who can't keep a job may be perfectly intelligent and well intentioned, but has a brain that can't process what he sees or hears well enough to follow instructions. It isn't enough to call these people jerks or masochists or losers, as seems to be the trend these days. Any discussion of their behavior must include the fact that each may have any one of a hundred built-in psychological disorders or deficiencies that can be treated—sometimes in short order.

The Marriage of Mind and Matter

All this said, we can illustrate the marriage of psychology and biology with the marriage of the Balusteris. Conventional wisdom and traditional writing about couples like George and Jennine emphasize only the psychological issues—the effects of childhood trauma, identification with parents, adult psychological styles, and so on. Thus George's irritability, temperamental explosiveness, and sullen negativity are explained as reactions to his early experiences with parents and siblings, the major details of which are as follows. George was the youngest by ten years of three children. Katarina Balusteri, their mother, was by all reports a vituperative tyrant who ran her home by brute personal force and cold-blooded emotional blackmail. She bullied and demeaned her husband and children when she was with them, and character-assassinated them when she wasn't. Guy Balusteri, George's father, was a timid man living in fear of his wife's tantrums and scoldings—cowering and accommodating in her presence and hurrying and scurrying in her absence to clean the house, cook the

* * *

After 1950, more and more psychiatric researchers gave up on doctoring their psychological theories to cover stubborn clinical facts and began to develop a set of biological models to help account for them—especially for the more serious psychiatric conditions. As I've emphasized repeatedly, these models were intended to balance the purely psychological points of view, not to replace them altogether. Progress in the biological realm was made on three fronts—classification of psychiatric disorders, research on brain mechanisms, and treatment of the disorders. Work in each area has been remarkably productive, and together account nicely for the kinds of problems on which the earlier psychological models had run aground.

I imagine that many people seeking a better relationship would rather just get on with it and not spend time on the details of psychiatric classification, let alone of brain science or biochemistry. That's fine. Skipping the next section will let you escape the details without missing anything useful about relationships. Or you can go right to the final section of this chapter, which returns to purely interpersonal matters. But if you'd like a little more background about your brain and how it can serve or abuse you and your relationships, the following will interest you.

Some Details of Distress

First, classification. Until the last few decades, understanding of the sorts of problems that plagued George and Jennine was based almost entirely on the sort of psychological theories I've just mentioned. As psychiatrists found the theories and the treatments based on them increasingly inadequate (especially for serious disorders like depression or schizophrenia), they stopped trying to explain the symptoms and started to work empirically. That is, they collected and organized their observations of psychological symptoms without preconceived notions about what caused them. Having collected the data, they used statistical methods to identify sets of symptoms that appeared repeatedly in a large number of people. These clusters of symptoms were called psychiatric syndromes (or disorders).

The syndromes were found in a range of people for whom

everything else varied widely (age, temperament, intelligence, social circumstances, and so on). The situation is like that in general medicine—if each of a number of people, however different from the others, has a runny nose, sore throat, fever, cough, all lasting only a few days, we say that each has a cold. We define the syndrome, cold, independent of what causes it, and then try to find out what causes it and what can be done about it. In psychiatry, if each of a large group of people has some or all of the following list of complaints, we say that he has a depressive syndrome: low mood, loss of interest in anything life has to offer, low self-esteem, agitation, difficulty with concentration and memory, tearfulness, disturbed sleep and appetite, hopelessness about the future, and so on. Usually a minimum number of symptoms from the list over a specific period of time is required for the diagnosis.

This is a radical departure from the purely psychological approach in which we started off assuming we know the cause of the trouble—George, for example, was blustery because of his identification with his mother, depressed because of anger turned inward, and so on. Radical changes of emphasis like this (paradigm changes, formally) always cause civil war. Tribal wars like the ones I described at McLean gripped the whole mental health field as the third edition of the American Psychiatric Association's diagnostic manual (DSM-III) came out in the early eighties. The earlier two editions had been organized on the older, purely psychological paradigms. DSM-III was the first manual to use the empirically statistical approach. Conservative forces scoffed at DSM-III or ignored it.

Nonetheless, the new approach soon became *the* approach, largely because of the unprecedented advances in brain research and treatment. What's been found is that specific areas and circuitry in the brain carry out specific functions—from routine activity like control of appetite or sexuality, to symbolic activity like language or arithmetic, to emergency functions like running from danger or wincing from pain.

One of the most intriguing findings is that a set of at least four systems regulates a wide range of brain functions relevant to almost all of psychiatry. Each of these systems uses a specific chemical synthesized in specific locations (in the brain stem) that activates and regulates a number of brain systems. Each chemical is transported to the appropriate brain areas, where it regulates the cell-to-cell communications that carry out the activities of those areas. These regulatory chemicals are dopamine, norepinephrine, serotonin, and acetylcholine—compounds we hear so much about these days in terms of their role in sleep or appetite control (serotonin), memory (acetylcholine), and so on. Because of this they're called neuromodulators—a subset of the general class of neurotransmitters, which includes any of a hundred or so compounds that carry signals between cells.

The seminal discovery of the last several decades has been that for each of the major psychiatric syndromes, a specific part (or parts) of the brain (or set of circuits between these parts) malfunctions. And in each case, one (or at most a few) of the neuromodulator chemicals is either deficient or present in excess in that part of the brain. Hence the popular term chemical imbalance as the basis of biologically based mental disorders. Imbalances in serotonin and norepinephrine, for example, underlie depressive disorders. Imbalances in dopamine underlie attention deficit disorder and schizophrenia. Deficiency in the acetylcholine system seems to underlie Alzheimer's disease. Anxiety disorders involve another chemical, GABA (gamma-aminobutyric acid), though in a different way from how the neuromodulators are involved in the other disorders (the differences don't matter for us).

For each condition, a person's brain makes either too little or too much of one of the compounds, or doesn't use it efficiently in the synapse—the gap between nerve cells. Thus, someone prone to an attentional disorder has too little dopamine or uses it inefficiently in the areas that regulate attention. The person with a mood disorder has the same problem with serotonin or norepinephrine (or both). A person with an anxiety disorder doesn't have enough GABA where he needs it. In a moment I'll suggest how these factors dovetail with psychological factors to generate the symptoms of the disorders.

The findings I've just summarized explain how psychiatric medications treat mental disorders. Therapeutic medications are compounds that block (or augment) the effects of the neuromodulator molecules when their level or activity are too high or too low. Therefore, administering these compounds brings brain function back into balance—thereby controlling the symptoms of the disorders. The research findings have also opened up a number of other ways to treat psychiatric syndromes.

Psychological Disorders as Susceptibilities to Stress

Probably the best way to think of the biological component of a psychiatric disorder is in terms of a susceptibility to develop that disorder under stress. Sometimes the stressors are specific; with depression, for example, it's usually some sort of loss or disappointment. Thus Jennine's brain chemistry was susceptible to imbalance in the face of a loss, and therefore to break down into a state of depression. For some people, like George, the susceptibility to depressive breakdown is so great that a depressive episode or a chronic state of depression can occur without any precipitating stress. For them, the ordinary pressure of daily life is enough to throw their system out of balance. A person with relatively normal brain chemistry, on the other hand, will have at most a mild depressive reaction to stressors that would bring out the full symptoms of depression in George or Jennine. The milder reaction would include sadness, lack of energy and enthusiasm, poor concentration, mental slowing, and so on—but not the full range or intensity of symptoms in a major depressive episode.

It's the same for the other disorders. In general, they represent excessive activation of a set of normal, automatic reactions. A panic attack, for example, is an excessive activation of the normal anxiety reaction to the threat of danger—the flight-or-fight response. In the same way, obsessions or compulsions are excessively intense, persistent activation of everyday routines and rituals that keep us from wasting too much time and energy on stopping to think through every little thing we do. These include things like remembering to turn off the stove, to look both ways before crossing a street, or, if we're raising children, to check chairs or car seats for half-eaten bananas, pet turtles, or sharp-edged toys before sitting down. With obsessions or compulsions, one or more routines like these get out of control and become pathologically intense and persistent.

In each of these cases it's mainly the brain chemistry that determines how much stress is needed to precipitate a disorder. Some people need little or no stress to develop full-blown syndromes, while others need stress of catastrophic proportions. Now, I'm not saying that psychological factors like traumatic childhood experiences don't contribute to susceptibility to the major disorders. I'm not even saying that traumatic childhood experiences don't cause permanent biochemical changes that contribute to our susceptibility to later psychiatric problems—it's likely that they do. Nonetheless, research and clinical experience show that the susceptibility is primarily biochemical and inborn.

The Effects of Stress: The Details

Exactly how stress can precipitate a specific psychiatric disorder is an intriguing question. Likewise, it's intriguing to consider how words, whether those used in talking therapy or in the delivery of threatening or saddening messages, can precipitate stress—which in turn can precipitate a psychiatric disorder. Fundamental questions like these (the kind seven-year-olds torment us with) are always the hardest—but over the last few years some answers are emerging. I'll mention some of these in the following paragraphs. Readers who want to stay with purely psychological material should skip these and go directly to page 29.

How a specific stress precipitates a specific disorder is probably best understood for depression. To understand this, we borrow a concept from neurology—that of disinhibition. Baby mammals, including humans, have a set of reflexes that help orient them to their mothers' breast, and then to suck at the nipple. These include the grasp reflex (grasping for an object that touches the hand), the snout reflex (puckering the lips when they're tapped), and a number of others. Specific neural circuits are preprogrammed to carry out these activities at specific times in development. I'll call these primary circuits. As the animals grow and move away from the mother's breast, the reflexes are suppressed, or inhibited, and remain inhibited throughout life. This inhibitory action is carried out by specific circuits I'll call secondary. A typical example is the grasp reflex. If you stroke the palm of a baby's hand, it closes around your finger. This reflex evolved to help the immature animal not yet able to hold on to its mother intentionally to grab on automatically. This reflex is mediated by the primary circuits. As the animal develops the capacity to hold on intentionally, the reflex is suppressed—an action mediated by the secondary circuits. In human babies the reflex is usually suppressed during the first half year of life.

Late in life, during the brain degeneration of senility (technically speaking, dementia), however, the inhibiting circuits fail earlier than those of the infantile reflexes, thereby allowing the earlier reflexes to re-emerge. It's a general tendency for circuits developed later to degenerate earlier. Neurologists use this process to test for degeneration of the central nervous system—if the grasp and other early reflexes are present in an adult, it indicates that the secondary reflexes have failed, and the secondary circuits are probably degenerating.

Beyond the simple reflexes I've just mentioned, young mammals have a set of much more complex behaviors that are pre-wired to operate at specific times for specific tasks. Especially relevant to depressive disorders are behaviors activated in a young animal when it's separated from its mother. At first it cries in protest, wildly seeking its mother, but after a while it goes into a state of shutdown. It remains immobile, eats little, sleeps little (to keep its eyes open for spotting mother), and utters a distinctive cry for its mother—all symptoms (in humans) of an agitated, and then a withdrawn, sort of depression. Recent imaging and electroencephalographic (EEG) work has identified the specific circuits involved.

As we'll see, loss is usually the precipitant for a depressive episode. The experience of loss is itself a product of processes in the cerebral cortex and in deeper (subcortical) areas—these processes in turn correspond to a complex pattern of firings between neurons. How this works is still somewhat mysterious, but we do know that as a result of the experience of loss, specific circuits are activated that generate the negative and self-critical feelings of depression. In normal times (no depression), these circuits are inhibited by other pre-wired circuits. When a serious enough loss is experienced, however, activity in the primary circuits breaks through the inhibitory control of the secondary circuits. People are susceptible to depression whose inhibitory circuitry fails during times when the primary circuitry is activated by loss. This is because of either insufficient neuromodulation or inefficient use of neuromodulator molecules in the synapse (or both). Someone whose inhibitory circuits are intact experiences a normal grief reaction in the face of a loss, while someone whose circuits aren't adequate experiences a depressive episode.

Similar circuit theories have been worked out for obsessive-compulsive disorder, ADD, and schizophrenia, and probably will be worked out for many other of the disorders discussed in this book.

The capacity of the brain to integrate incoming signals and generate a theme—here, that of loss—is central to a number of processes relating to emotional disorders. Once the brain has integrated its inputs and generated the theme of danger, for example, it signals the brain stem dopamine centers to activate those dopamine-driven circuits that mediate the flight-or-fight reflex. If this system is activated overzealously, the result is a panic attack. If it's activated chronically, the result is a chronic anxiety state.

This scheme, by the way, helps explain how talking therapy can make changes in patients with serious disorders like depression or schizophrenia. We've seen that as they gather sensory input, a collection of cortical and subcortical brain centers can activate the brain stem neuromodulatory centers. In depression, for example, brain stem centers adjust the circuitry responsible for both the generation (with the primary circuits) and suppression (secondary circuits) of symptoms. We can therefore imagine that the patterns of cortical and subcortical firings related to specific concepts that are handled in psychotherapy can adjust the circuits back toward the inhibition of depressive experience. The discussion between therapist and patient represents a set of trials and errors aimed at finding those firing patterns that adjust the circuitry back to normal. It's thus an ongoing biofeedback process—one that in the case of talking therapy unfortunately changes the circuits very slowly.

Understanding as we do a good deal about the biological aspects of the disorders that most disturb interpersonal relations does not minimize the role of psychological factors. Instead, it brings balance into our understanding of what these disorders do to people and relationships. George and his siblings, for example, all had endured Katarina as children. But George's biochemistry was the most susceptible to her influence, and made his reactions to her and the pain he felt because of her more intense than those of the others. Because of this he developed a personality style that helped him deal with her and the pain she caused him, one that relied on the psychological maneuvers of identification with the aggressor and the turning of anger inward. His brother and sister, less susceptible to feeling hurt by their mother, could develop personalities without such dramatic modes of self-protection—and therefore became much more personable.

Armed with these ideas, we can now understand that the reason that George's personality changed so strikingly after marriage was a combination of both psychological and biological factors. First, and purely psychological, was that he was now close, emotionally and physically, to a woman he loved—and was therefore vulnerable to her. Because of this he feared (deep down) that she would treat him as his mother had. He therefore defended himself in advance from this possibility with his maladaptive defenses. Since his fear (and the protective maneuvers it motivated) were kept well out of awareness (unconscious, in Freudian terms), he wasn't able to measure it against the reality of Jennine's harmlessness—and therefore to be able to discard it as unnecessary. Second, and more purely biological, was that when children of any age leave home for the first time, they feel a good deal of distress (separation anxiety, technically speaking). This anxiety disrupts the chemical balances in the specific brain areas that cope with separation and loss. Since George's brain didn't regulate these reactions very well, the system got out of balance and a depression followed.

Biology, Psychology, and Relationships

Now that we've mixed together some ideas about the brain and its biology with some ideas about psychology, what does this have to do with relationships? Everything. As we first learned from

Dawn in the Introduction, nothing ambushes a relationship like a psychiatric disorder. But what if you don't have major psychiatric problems?

First, although there are strict criteria for the major disorders, a great many of us have minor variants of them—less severe dysregulations of our chemical systems, to use the ideas I've been developing here. Thus what I'm going to say throughout the book about the effect on relationships of the major disorders applies to a much wider range of people than just those who meet the criteria of the diagnostic manuals.

Second, and even more sobering, is that even discounting minor variants, there would still be a very high likelihood that one of the full-blown syndromes is affecting your life. This is because they're very common, and because there's a large number of them. Thus the likelihood of either partner in any relationship having one of the disorders is quite high. To show this, we can consider the prevalence of seven of the disorders that most commonly disrupt relationships. If we assign approximate percentages reported in the psychiatric literature for people susceptible to these disorders, we can compute the likelihood of any couple having at least one member affected by one of the full-blown disorders. The percentage of people susceptible to them are as follows: mood disorders (20 percent), obsessive-compulsive disorder (2 percent), generalized anxiety disorder (5 percent), specific phobia (10 percent), agoraphobia (fear of open places) (2 percent), dysthymia (chronic depression) (6 percent), and attention deficit disorder (10 percent). Assuming that the disorders themselves don't affect the ways people choose their partners, these percentages correspond to a likelihood of around 65 percent that any relationship has at least one partner with at least one of these disorders. I've left out social phobia (13 percent of the population) and schizotypical personality (7 percent of the population)—discussed in Chapters Four and Seven, respectively—because, as we'll see, they're more likely to keep people out of relationships altogether rather than to disturb ongoing relationships.

The following three chapters discuss in detail the disorders I've just listed. The emphasis is on how these disorders distress and disrupt interpersonal relationships. We'll see that the set of symptoms and character traits for each disorder give it a particular set of ways to undermine, or preclude, gratifying and ongoing relationships.

CHAPTER 2

Attention Deficit Disorder and Interpersonal Relationships

To anyone who's survived a serious depression or panic attack, the extent of public ignorance about these conditions is bewildering. For attentional disorders, however, the situation is even worse. With depression or anxiety, even people with no understanding of their various forms understand the feelings. With disorders of attention, on the other hand, neither the people who suffer from them, or those who don't, seem to know anything about them. Most people, including many psychiatrists (*most,* until just a few years ago), don't know that many ADD children never outlive the disorder. As adults, they feel stupid, lazy, or otherwise inferior—because all their lives people have been telling them that they are. This chapter describes this very common disorder in both children and adults and offers some ways to deal with it. It explains how to recognize ADD in an adult, either in yourself or in someone you care about, and then how to cope with the problems that ADD brings.

Defining the Problem

What are these disorders, then? In general the syndrome is one of distractibility, impulsivity, and hyperactivity, though there may not be any hyperactivity, especially in adults. It is much more common in boys—estimates range from four to nine times as many boys as girls—and is usually evident within the first few years of life.

The prototypic ADD child is unmistakable. His attention jumps off task at the slightest interruption: a voice across the room, someone entering the doorway, or just a passing thought that turns into a daydream. His teachers complain of his daydreaming in class, and attribute this to a lack of interest in the material rather than to the built-in inability to concentrate that in fact causes the condition. His impulsivity makes him leap into activities, literally and figuratively, without giving a thought to possible consequences: He'll jump into a pool without knowing how to swim, run into the street without looking, or yield to an irresistible urge to run to the head of any line. His hyperactivity, if present, is a persistent fidgetiness: He'll get up and sit down over and over, bounce his legs continuously, look around, and wiggle and wriggle so constantly that thirty years later the term "wiggleworm" will bring an embarrassed smile (or frown) of reminiscence. He is always interrupting, spilling his milk, dropping things, talking out of turn, losing his homework, or breaking his toys.

In class, he can't keep his mind on his work: His attention wanders when the teacher talks to the class or when he tries to read—an activity that for many ADHD children involves running their eyes over and over a page without anything sticking in their minds. Change is difficult for someone with ADD—like starting or stopping any activity, including going from sleep to wakefulness. Thus, it's very difficult to get children (or adults) with ADD out of bed in the morning. On top of all this, his endless fidgeting, interrupting, hitting, talking, joking, crying, fighting, and screaming can waste most of a school year for a whole class of students, thereby having his parents and those of the other children at one another's throats. All the while he's breaking the district's budget on his special needs for tutoring and extra discipline.

All this takes a terrible toll on his self-esteem. This may be the most pernicious aspect of the disorder—whether or not the condition persists into adulthood. Constantly messing up everything he tries and continually provoking the exasperation and criticism of parents, teachers, and friends, he soon sees himself as a loser. At the same time, he knows that there's something wrong with his mind. He knows that other children can listen to the teacher or to one another, can read their lessons and remember to do their homework—but he can't do any of these things no matter how hard he tries. He leaves childhood feeling defective and incompetent, a self-image that persists all his life.

For a long time, what we knew about attentional disorders was confused by an overemphasis on hyperactivity. This is understandable to anyone who's seen a hyperactive ADD (so-called ADHD) child or adult, because the constant fidgeting and daredevil theatrics are so overt. In most cases the hyperactivity ceases during adolescence. Because of this, it was once thought that the attention problems go away at the same time. This was a great error that left undiagnosed and untreated a tremendous number of people, who continued to have trouble paying attention to a world that got more complex every year.

Psychiatry has only recently discovered the inaccuracy of this point of view; an explosion of articles, books, lectures, and talk show appearances is now providing a good deal of information and comfort to adults still suffering from ADD. There are millions of adults with ADD. As with any psychiatric disorder, their personalities, temperaments, and lifestyles differ tremendously, but the symptom list (or parts of it) is repeated in each case.

How an adult with ADD turns out seems to depend on the severity of his disorder, on his talent and intelligence, and to a large degree on blind luck (what his family is like, what his teachers were like, what activities are available that let him excel despite his problems, what opportunities for delinquency and crime presented themselves). A number of extremely successful people have ADD, but have used their talents and interpersonal skills to surround themselves with an entourage of loyal assistants to keep them organized. At the other end of the spectrum are people who are chronically homeless or in jails and prisons because they've been unable to surmount the severe limitations ADD imposes on what they can do to succeed in life.

Like the child with ADD, the adult has trouble focusing his

attention and is too impulsive for his own good. Only rarely, however, is he physically hyperactive. Distractibility is the hallmark: Whether in conversations, at lectures, or trying to read, his mind wanders off continually. Some distractions are external: In a room full of people his attention bounces from person to person to the point that he's so overwhelmed with stimuli that he can't function, and he often leaves the room in a near panic. Some distractions are internal: His mind is continually jumping to memories or fantasies that take him away from the thought or task at hand. As paradoxical as it sounds, sometimes the problem is that he focuses too deeply: Some ADD sufferers can get lost in a task for hours on end, losing complete contact with the world around them. Computer tasks (or games) and TV shows can so capture an ADD person's attention that he's barely responsive to the outer world.

Impulsivity is the second defining trait of ADD. Things have to happen now. If someone with ADD wants an appointment, for example, it has to be today—despite the fact that he's procrastinated about calling for two years. In the same way that an ADD child will jump into a swimming pool without knowing how to swim, an adult with ADD will leap into schemes and enterprises without knowing what's involved or what the consequences are likely to be.

An important characteristic of adults with ADD that is particularly harmful to relationships is that they become bored very easily—with both things and people. Distractibility and impulsiveness contribute to these traits, but on a more fundamental level they're the result of a difficulty sustaining ideas and mental images over periods of time. In the very short term the problem is that thoughts and images continually evaporate and are quickly replaced by other, often completely unrelated, ideas or images. This leads to the characteristic scattered thought processes and easy distractibility. Over longer periods the problem is that interests fade more rapidly than for people without ADD. Thus the person jumps from activity to activity and from person to person in what looks like inconstancy and fickleness to anyone without ADD, and like natural exuberance or high standards for partners or other rationalizations to the person with ADD. In the long term the problem is a difficulty maintaining the image of a beloved person over the years—that is, sustaining a set of loving feelings and an attitude of loyalty toward that person. This is especially difficult in the face of the inevitable stresses any relationship faces over time. The non-ADD half of a couple often senses the fragility of his partner's attachment, and is continuously insecure about his place in his partner's affections.

ADD and Communication

The effect of ADD on communication may be its most troublesome aspect and deserves a section of its own. The syndrome produces a number of distinctive patterns of disturbed communication, which I'll try to make recognizable to people with ADD and to those who try to talk with them (like their partners). The symptoms disrupt both listening and being listened to. Naturally enough, inattention and distractibility prevent a person from hearing all of what's said to him. A person with ADD can capture a substantial part of any message only with a great deal of effort—and, as we'll see in a moment, the effort has its own disruptive effects on communication. ADD also disrupts how a person communicates to someone else. For one thing, continual distractions make what he says, however intelligent, difficult to follow—especially to people with an orderly, linear style of thinking and listening. To make things worse, in many people with ADD there's an irresistible pressure to interrupt constantly. They know, even if only subliminally, that if something occurs to them, they'd better say it now or else it evaporates, so they just blurt it out. This adds irritation to incoherence and leads many people to avoid someone with ADD altogether.

In some people with ADD there is a concrete or literal quality to their thinking that can make communication even more confusing. Some, for example, don't catch on to humor very well, and this leads to confusion and awkward pauses in conversation. Others seem unusually literal, and get lost if someone uses a metaphor or other figure of speech. Still others simply don't draw the conclusions that seem obvious to anyone else. A young woman that a patient of mine was starting to date warned him that if he didn't bring along six chaperones on their next date, she was going to climb all over him when she got him home. Since he often worried that women didn't like him, I remarked that this woman, at least, did seem attracted to him. "Why do you say that?" he asked me in as sober a deadpan as if he were trying to be terribly witty—but he wasn't. Another patient, a very intelligent software engineer, on telling me that he'd answered yes to ninety-eight of a hundred questions on a self-administered test for ADD, was completely baffled when I responded, well, it sounds pretty likely that you have ADD.

Another pattern I call *communication by strobe light.* A strobe light, you'll recall, flashes briefly at short intervals, thereby momentarily stopping the action it illuminates (the effect is especially dramatic in a dark room). You can do the same thing by repeatedly blinking your eyes when you're looking at, say, the hubcap of a spinning car wheel. For the instant between blinks, the wheel seems to stand still. Thus the motion of the wheel looks like a series of still shots, a significant distortion of what it's really doing. Unfortunately, ADD causes a similar distortion of how a person hears what people say to him. From the continuous stream of language, a set of "stills" is picked out, and the rest is lost in the many periods of inattention. The gaps are then filled in with whatever the person imagines was said. Thus what he thinks he heard is a mix of what he did hear and what he imagines he heard. The result can be very far from what was actually said, especially when the conversation is emotionally charged. In that case the person's psychological agendas, wishes, and fears are strongly activated and therefore especially likely to distort communication by inserting themselves into the gaps between "stills."

Even when a person works to suppress his inattention, the effort itself makes trouble. One way people with ADD focus is by applying brute psychological force—they mobilize a great deal of energy to stay locked on to whatever's being said to them. The intensity, however, confuses listeners. A typical example occurred when I introduced myself to one of my older daughter's teachers. I was distressed by her response—or, rather, by the apparent lack of response. With complete objectivity, you understand, I'd expected the declaration that I was Katie's father to provoke an immediate expression of reverence for that remarkable young lady. Her teacher, however, simply looked at me as if she couldn't remember who Katie was (unthinkable), or maybe as if she thought I was strange (somewhat thinkable), or any of a thousand other ludicrous manifestations of my own fears and concerns. I in turn felt rather imposed on. It wasn't until she asked me some weeks later whether ADD fades with age—and acknowledged that she'd been a hyperactive child—that I understood that she'd simply been exerting her habitual degree of intensity in order to focus when meeting someone.

The effect can be disconcerting, even amusing—if you don't mind laughing at yourself a bit for your initial reactions. A twenty-seven-year-old woman with severe ADD threw me for a loop when she first sat down in my office. She was unusually attractive, and the searching way she gazed at me initially gave me a jolt of flattered pleasure. In reality, she was simply trying to focus on what I was saying—all the while, in fact, repeating it to herself as I spoke. This was something that she'd learned helped her assimilate what was said to her. Her astonishment that with treatment she no longer had to do this was a pleasure to behold, and matched my own momentary astonishment in that initial instant when she seemed to look at me with such instantaneous adoration.

Other Effects on Relationships

Because distractibility, impulsiveness, and difficulty communicating interfere with almost everything it takes to succeed both at work and in relationships, adults with ADD are usually underachievers in both areas. By adulthood they usually can maintain their attention for longer periods, but this takes a great deal of energy. Typically a person with ADD maintains interest in an activity for a period of days or weeks (not seconds or minutes like a child), but then runs out of steam. Thus he doesn't have the perseverance to get through the training needed for a profession. Some do get through training and carry out challenging jobs, but they have to expend a great deal of energy keeping themselves centered. Some can do this by recruiting an entourage of helpers, but this works only for people with the talent or intelligence required to command such cooperation. People with less talent typically find career niches in which their limitations don't disrupt their work, but these are usually well beneath their capacity.

However well they do in life, this accumulation of failure and underachievement leads to an awful image of oneself. No matter how well ADD sufferers have done, there have always been things they couldn't do like everyone else—read, persevere, communicate. This leads to a sense that they've gotten by on the basis of stealth, or charm, or other sleight of hand, so to speak, rather than by good hard work like everyone else. Because of this, a person with ADD feels like a *fraud*, always having to shield his incapacities with clever but usually unreliable ways. This is an unfortunate sense of oneself to have to carry around, and over time it adds further misery to the ordeal of going through life with ADD.

Most adults with ADD don't have the combination of talent, communication skills, and good luck to find a career niche that accommodates their deficits. One group does especially poorly. All through school they were unable to keep up, and later at work their impulsiveness and inability to concentrate led to repeated conflicts and dismissals. Many adjust by getting into activities that provide quick rewards without requiring persistence, preparation or concentration—like drug abuse or criminal activity. Sometimes this is simply an attempt to escape from their confusing, frustrating, and (to their minds) boring lives, but other times it's more troublesome because it works *too* well. For some people with ADD, that is, using illicit stimulants like amphetamines, cocaine, or even caffeine relieves the ADD symptoms. Many find that they feel calm or normal only when they're on one of these drugs. Other people feel the same effect with marijuana. Marijuana seems to intensify sensation generally, and for these people it seems to intensify the capacity to focus. Unfortunately, the marijuana or stimulants found on the street vary in quality and purity. Thus they're hard to use in any consistent way, and most people who try *using* illicit substances to self-medicate their ADD eventually wind up *abusing* them. The drug abuse and criminal activity very often land people with ADD in jail or prison. Estimates have been made that up to seventy or eighty percent of the prison population suffers from ADD.

The adult with ADD, then, is impulsive, distractible, a little unusual in his thought processes, and has an awful self-image.

Whatever he has in mind—whether it's something he's thinking or hearing or reading, or something he's intending to do or say—seems to evaporate too fast, leaving him at the mercy of whatever catches his eye or pops into his head. This makes it hard to stay in contact with him well enough or long enough to form a viable relationship. To make things worse, all his life he's felt fraudulent and inadequate—which certainly makes it hard to present himself to someone in the hope of starting a relationship.

To illustrate the problems ADD can bring to a relationship, I'll introduce Wendell Satterly, whose marriage and career were adversely affected by his ADD. In the final section I'll turn to the practical matters of what to do if you suspect that you may have ADD yourself, how to spot someone who has ADD, and, if you're attracted to him, how to avoid his disrupting your life. I'll leave the more complicated problems of entering or negotiating a relationship with someone with ADD to Chapters Five to Seven—which will explain how to avoid a relationship with the wrong person and how to maintain one with the right person.

The Case of the Mad Professor Satterly

Dr. Satterly came to my office shortly after he turned fifty. He was a literature professor at a local junior college, married, and miserable. His marriage had begun to unravel shortly after it began, though he and his wife had stayed together by the grace of what he called his wife's saintliness—and what anyone else would call a blend of love, stubbornness, and masochism. In recent months, however, the reservoir of these virtues had run dry, and in recent weeks the relationship had fallen apart completely. Mrs. Satterly had left him, taking their ten-year-old son with her. The immediate precipitant was her discovery of Satterly's months-long affair with her sister.

"She was like France," he said of his sister-in-law, "no spring, no fall, no morals," expecting, somehow, that I knew what he meant. His humor, it seemed, was like everything else about him: obscure, idiosyncratic, as if without point or direction. The rest of the story, about his sister-in-law and about everything else in his life, needed constant refocusing and clarifying for me to make sense of it. It quickly became clear that he was a very intelligent man, unusually gifted verbally, but that he had absolutely no organization to his narration and no control over his behavior. Jean, his sister-in-law, was but the latest in a very long list of women, mostly students and fellow teachers, who found him attractive if quirky, told him so, and were accepted on the spot as his lover of the moment. He said that he found their approval (which he assumed accompanied the attraction) irresistible; he was, therefore, a chronic pushover for anyone who wanted him.

Its meandering presentation aside, the story left me puzzled. He was attractive, intelligent, and gifted (especially with poetry: He could produce odes or sonnets to illustrate his narrative at the drop of an allusion, and cite Shakespeare, Milton, and many others I barely knew). It was hardly surprising that women would be drawn to him. Yet his reaction each time this happened was such surprise and gratitude that, as I said, he could resist no unreasonable offer. Somehow, I told him, he must have decided that women didn't like him; I asked him how this came about. His answer confirmed the diagnosis of ADD that I'd reached based on his scattered, if brilliant, style of thought.

An only child, he'd been trouble right from the start. His parents maintain that he'd spent twenty years in his terrible twos. From nursery school to his last year in college, that is to say, he never sat still, paid attention, or stopped talking in class. His talent, creativity, and intelligence, however, continually rescued him from academic disaster. Graduate school, though, with its loose structure and preoccupation with talent and potential, was a haven, so much so that he spent twelve years there trying to organize his work enough to complete a doctorate. Finally, with the help of the woman he later married, he got his work in shape, completed his dissertation, and became Dr. Satterly.

After he finished his degree, Wendell and Marion got married. His new wife felt sure that with her inspiration and organization he would succeed brilliantly. But it never happened. Since that time he'd taught at the junior college level, though it was clear to all who knew his capacity that he should have risen much higher in academia. He could not, however, focus his research on any one subject or complete any literary project, so that in the publish-or-perish world of scholastic endeavor, he could never flourish.

The greatest casualty of Satterly's checkered career was his self-esteem. As a child he was a fumbling, clumsily unathletic kid barely tolerated by his classmates. He could never throw a ball "within a stanza" of his target, he said with his usual opaque imagery. As an adolescent he felt he was perpetually on the verge of puberty: awkward with the girls, laughed at by the boys, and constantly exasperating his teachers, who resented his inattention and inability to sit still for their presentations. He had a steady girlfriend for two years in college, but on proposing marriage he was mortified when she told him that she was pregnant by someone else and intended to marry him. From that disaster until meeting his wife, he never pursued a liaison beyond a one-or two-night stand; he agreed to marry Marion only after a several-years-long campaign on her part.

At fifty, then, Satterly felt like a failure on all fronts. At the heart of the matter was his sense that he had never been able to control himself, mentally or physically. He knew that other people could sit down, concentrate, and be productive—but he had no idea how to be more like them. As long as his wife was with him, her admiration sustained his faith in himself. Over the last few months, though, she was losing patience with him. He felt that she was ready to leave him, and the thought shattered him. He confided this to his wife's sister, Jean, hoping that she could help him back into his wife's good graces. Unbeknownst to the supremely inattentive Satterly, however, Jean had all her life resented her brighter and more attractive younger sister, and was all too happy to take advantage of the circumstance. The rest we know.

Finishing his story, he asked if I would meet with his wife. He hoped that I could help discover what had changed in her feelings, and what, if anything, he could do about it. I agreed to interview her. As I listened to her description of recent events, it seemed that she too had no idea why her tolerance for her husband's idiosyncracies had run out—even before the affair with Jean. She could only suggest that the stress of raising their son might have drained her.

I asked what was so stressful about raising the boy, and was not at all surprised by her answer. Wyatt was wriggly, inattentive, talkative, impossible to discipline, brilliant, and loved poetry. He was also clumsy at athletics, called a nerd by his classmates, and felt like a loser. His mother was heartbroken; she recognized the father in the son, of course, and though she tried to resist blaming him for it, she couldn't help feeling that in some way it *was* his fault. She had no idea that ADHD was a biological condition that the son had inherited from his father—and not the result of her son imitating his father or of Wendell's inadvertent instructions in scatterbrainedness (as her girlfriends hypothesized). Thus her suffering from her son's difficulties, and her feeling that her husband had somehow caused them, had worn away her tolerance and eventually her love. Her sister's betrayal was only the last rub.

The son was treated by a child psychiatrist, and he improved remarkably. Aside from mild clumsiness and a hopeless ineptitude at mathematics (going back several paternal generations), he emerged a perfectly normal and very bright fifth-grader. I also treated the father; his response was slower and less complete, but there was a significant change in his focus, organization, and productivity. Within a few months he finished a text on sixteenth-century English poetry, a burden he'd carried for two decades of fumbling and disorganized attempts to prepare it for publication.

It would be wonderful to add that the Satterlys' marriage was resurrected by these efforts, but it wasn't. Things had gone too far for Marion; she wanted to start again without the burden of dealing with Wendell, no matter how much he'd improved. She was sad about this, but felt that she would get past it and in time do much better. Wendell was more philosophical, and felt it was all for the best. If it weren't for his ADD, he said, he'd never have married Marion and had their many years together—and they'd never have had Wyatt (who was the light of his life). And if Marion hadn't left, the boy might have waited much longer for treatment, and, like his father, have done much less well for the delay.

"It was a strange fashion of forsaking," he said of the divorce on our last meeting, and I suppose he meant something by that.

Practical Lessons: What to Do If You Think You're the Satterlys

The plight of the Satterlys shows that whether you have ADD or are dealing with someone who has it, what you don't know about the disorder will indeed hurt you. What you need to know depends on which predicament you're in—potential patient or potential partner. We'll avoid these one predicament at a time.

What to Do If You Think You're Wendell

If you've read this far and suspect you have ADD, you're already past the biggest hurdle: considering the possibility and taking it seriously. The next thing to do is reread pages 34 and 35 and see if you recognize yourself as a child. Since people with ADD often don't remember their childhood too well, you may have to ask your parents, siblings, or friends what they remember. What you (or they) need to recall is:

Were you the sort of kid who was easily bored in class (no matter how challenging or interesting the material) and found your mind continually wandering off?

Did your report cards say that you have potential but need to apply yourself? Or that you daydream in class?

Were you always in trouble for talking in class, getting out of your seat, or forgetting assignments?

Was it hard to read assignments without your mind wandering off?

Did how you succeed in a class depend a great deal on how much you liked the teacher (and therefore how hard you worked to pay attention)?

In my experience, adult women with ADD don't always report the sort of childhood symptoms just mentioned. Thus it's important not to rule out ADD in a woman just because her childhood wasn't as classically hyperactive, inattentive, or impulsive as it was for boys.

For adults with ADD, reading is often a good tip-off: Does your mind still wander when you read, no matter how hard you try to focus on the material? Does this make reading books an ordeal and make you prefer newspapers and magazines? (Many adults with ADD are good readers, and some hyperfocus when they read; thus if reading isn't a problem, you can't automatically rule out the diagnosis.) Other questions to ask yourself:

Does your mind wander off during other activities, like conversations, lectures, or even movies?

Do you find yourself getting lost when someone gives you complicated directions for doing something or getting somewhere (either during the directions or while trying to follow them)?

Do you find yourself procrastinating, and no degree of effort gets you past it (except the adrenaline rush just before a deadline)?

Do piles of papers, bills, lists, and magazines build up everywhere, and, try as you might, keep multiplying as if by spontaneous generation?

Do you make lists to get you organized, but then forget where you put them, or even if you can find them, that you can't decipher them?

Do you find that you do things piecemeal—like cleaning house by bouncing all around the place, fixing this, tidying that, cleaning the other thing, as various broken, messy, or dirty things catch your eye? Do you continually irritate people by forgetting to call them, by losing the things they lend you, or by otherwise flaking out on your responsibilities to them? Are you working very much beneath your potential because you can't put up with whatever training, red tape, or rules and regulations it would take to get you where, deep down, you'd love to be?

Drug use is often a big hint. Like reading, it's not diagnostic, but if you've dabbled in stimulants (cocaine, speed, crack, crank, even caffeine) or marijuana, and find that they calm or focus you, this is a hint. Do you drink cup after cup of coffee or chain-smoke cigarettes to keep yourself calm or focused? I met a man recently whose intelligence and multiple talents seemed incompatible with his history of taking and then quickly losing a series of low-level jobs. My confusion disappeared, however, when he mentioned that he'd been a bomber pilot in Vietnam, and, unlike his comrades, could not take amphetamines to stay awake on missions because they invariably put him to sleep.

* * *

Though it's hard to quantify such things, my experience has been that if there are even three or four yes answers to these questions, ADD is likely. Eight or ten yeses all but clinch the diagnosis. There are a number of things to do at this point. Since ADD is a neurological condition, eventually you'll need professional help—but before going to a specialist (and later, as you go), there are some commonsense things you can do to help you and your relationship.

Learning as much as you can about ADD, and teaching what you've learned to those around you, is especially important. As we've seen, simply understanding that much of your interpersonal trouble results from ADD (and from your accommodations to it) is remarkably therapeutic. You can learn from books, lectures, and especially from other people with ADD. Group therapy for people with ADD is very useful. People learn that they're not alone in their suffering, and learn how others have coped with the condition. If the significant people in your life, like your employer, teachers, business associates, your parents and children, and most important, your partner, don't know or understand enough about ADD, you'll have to explain it to them. You'll need to teach them the symptoms of ADD, its neurochemical basis, and how it's made trouble for you. This isn't easy. Most people are skeptical about things they've never heard of, and will worry that you're using this implausible-sounding new condition (or trendy fad) to deny responsibility for your actions, avoid work, and so on. I find that even the most sympathetic and enlightened employers and supervisors, unless they know about (or have) ADD, will need to watch your work improve for a while before they believe what you're saying. Therefore, put as much effort as you can into increasing organization, decreasing procrastination, and in communicating more clearly as your ADD is treated.

Providing organization and structure for yourself—both internally and externally—is very helpful for people with ADD, especially when combined with professional help. One way to add organization to your life is to do as much as you can on a fixed schedule. This frees you from having to remember to do things and to organize your days to fit them in—a good thing because remembering and organizing don't come easy for someone with

ADD. Do your laundry, for example, every Tuesday—and write it on a weekly calendar or in a day planner for every Tuesday. Likewise, things like paying rent, making insurance payments, and the like can be assigned specific times each week. Regular doctor's or dentist's appointments, classes or club meetings, can be routinized in this way. Over time they become as automatic as any other learned habits like dotting an i or stopping at a red light. The more lists, reminder notes, appointment books, to-do lists, calendars, the better.

Organization must also be built into your approach to activities. Don't, for example, put paperwork, bills, or other items that demand timely responses into piles on your desk marked "To Do"—because you won't do them. You'll only make piles of paper everywhere, the bottom layers of which will have turned to coal long before you get to them. Develop, instead, the habit of handling each piece of paperwork as soon as you get it instead of putting it aside and then misplacing or forgetting about it as your mind wanders elsewhere. Likewise, develop the habit of subdividing complex tasks—like filing your taxes or planning a remodeling of your house—into subtasks. In this way you won't be overwhelmed by the enormity of the overall task, and instead can focus on one job at a time, like running through your checkbook for deductible items, rescuing receipts from your collection of piles, calling contractors, shopping for windows, and other bite-sized pieces of the big jobs that intimidate you.

Another part of providing suitable structure is arranging for special accommodations at work or in school. Tests in school, for example, or College Board Examinations can be given untimed, assignments can be individualized, and so on. It's probably more difficult to arrange accommodations in the bottom-line driven workplace, but you need to do it. Making your boss or supervisor as knowledgeable as possible about ADD is the way to start. Teach him how you need the structure of deadlines, regular assignments, and reviews, how you work better on a series of subtasks rather than on one large assignment that requires organizational ability well beyond you—his knowing all this can make a great difference.

There are several things you'll need to do that are purely interpersonal. You'll have to learn, for example, not to use ADD as an excuse, especially for what you've already done to hurt your relationship. It helps a relationship to learn to direct whatever anger you feel about the effects of your ADD at the ADD, not at yourself or your partner. It also helps to keep away from things you don't do well and stay with things you can do well. This will bolster your confidence and self-esteem. Likewise, try to spend time with people and groups who understand you, and to avoid those who don't or who criticize you for your ADD-related limitations. For keeping all these attitudes and activities in mind, many people find it useful to use a coach. It can be a friend, a relative, or a mental health professional. He can help remind you to do the things that control the ADD, and to avoid the ones that let the ADD control you—all the while providing a steady and reliable source of encouragement and understanding.

Ultimately, however, you will need professional help. ADD is a disorder of brain chemistry and, however you deal with it, it won't change without direct treatment of the chemical imbalances involved. If you absolutely hate even the idea of going to a psychiatrist, it may be best for you to talk to your family doctor or internist—but a good psychiatrist is the person with the training and experience in the area. A major drawback (especially if you go to a nonpsychiatrist or choose a psychiatrist at random) is that you're at the mercy of the doctor's prejudices and level of experience with ADD. It's best to ask around first and find who's had the most experience and the best results. Many psychiatrists and most nonmedical therapists don't know much about ADD. Also, too many professionals still think ADD is a fad (you should just buckle down and apply yourself, they think). Avoid them. A man with an unusually striking case of ADD was told by his internist that he didn't have ADD, he just wasn't very smart (his IQ tested at 141 before treatment). Potential sources of good referrals are self-help groups like CHADD (Children and Adults with Attention Deficit Disorders) that you can find listed at your local library, your county medical society, or the Internet.

If you're like most people, seeking help will take a good deal of willpower. You can help galvanize yourself into action by reminding yourself that you've done the hardest part of the work: getting to the point of admitting you need help and starting to look for it. Remind yourself, too, that the question that's haunted you your whole life—whether there's something wrong with your mind—is finally being answered, and the news isn't going to be as bad as you've feared. It isn't that you're lazy, stupid, or congenitally inadequate. And *it isn't your fault:* You have a physiological disorder, you've inherited it, you can get treated for it, and you're going to do a lot better. You'll also have to steel yourself to the fact that you're going to run into resistance both from uninformed professionals and from family and friends. Once you're treated for ADD, the results are usually gratifying enough that you won't mind criticism about what you're doing for yourself. But between the time you decide that you've probably got ADD and the moment you go in for help, you're at risk of being talked out of what you're doing.

As I said, everyone thinks he's an expert about the mind. To help avoid being talked out of what you know you need to do, I offer three things to keep in mind about bad advice. You can think of them as the three commandments of bad advice. Most people advising you about your ADD and its treatment will follow these religiously—and not just for ADD, but for all the disorders we'll consider. Remind yourself of this as you listen to what they say.

First, the less someone knows about something, the louder he carries on about it. People who know what they're talking about make their points gently and listen to how you respond. Second, when most people try to understand you, they start by imagining that you're exactly like them. Since this isn't too likely, they're almost always wrong about you. Third (and most troublesome), when faced with something he doesn't understand, a person understands it in the way that most makes him feel good about himself.

These items are the only explanation I have for how so many people, in complete ignorance about the brain and its workings, can insist, straight-faced and cold sober, that someone with ADD has nothing wrong with him but simply isn't as disciplined, hard-working, or generally excellent as they themselves happen to be. Don't argue with them. Simply thank them for trying to help (which, in fairness, they usually are), and then go to the best doctor you can find and tell him about all the yeses you answered to the list of questions a few paragraphs back. Then listen to what he says.

What to Do If You Think You're Marion

The other side of the coin is more difficult: deciding whether someone you're drawn to is too impaired by ADD to have a good relationship with you. This task involves a number of subtasks: (1) catching on that the person may have ADD, (2) finding out if the person is willing to consider the possibility and seek help if ADD is likely, and (3) deciding (whether or not the person gets help) whether he or she is able to deal with the ADD well enough to be in a relationship with you—that is, if what you like outweighs what's wrong.

Big Question #1: Does He Have ADD?

Spotting ADD in someone else involves the same questions the potential patient must ask about himself, but now the answers come from your perspective as someone who sees him from the outside. Questions about ADD that are easier to answer from the outside include the following: Is he a chronic underachiever, and if so, is it because he can't get himself organized, do things on time, or understand or cooperate with others? Does he get up a head of steam for a dozen projects at a time, only to forget or lose interest a few days or weeks down the line? Is it nearly impossible for him to get out of bed in the morning? Does he jump into any adventure that presents itself without thinking about the consequences? Does he seem good at getting you to organize him because he can't do it himself? All the questions from the "What if you think you're Wendell" section also apply, of course.

Big Question #2: Will He Get Help?

If you've come up with a number of yeses to the questions in the preceding paragraph, then you're a potential Marion Satterly. Now, this may not be such a bad thing (there's a lot to love about Wendell Satterly, after all), but think the matter through before you get into a relationship with someone like him. The absolutely worst thing you can do is to imagine that you can change him—especially without professional help. Even *with* professional help there are no guarantees that he'll change at all, especially in the way you'd like him to. If he isn't willing to consider the diagnosis of ADD, let alone see someone for help, then you'll have to decide if you can deal with him the way he is. If this is a new relationship, the sooner you decide, the better, because once you've gotten to know and care about someone, it's harder to think objectively about what's best for you.

Now, this sounds easier on paper than it is in reality. Telling someone you think there's something wrong with his brain takes courage—and tact—whether you're just getting to care about (or fall in love with) someone, or have loved him for years. Nonetheless, if you don't raise the topic, it will raise itself. Your new friend's distractibility and disorganization sooner or later will begin to erode the relationship, or your long-term partner's ADD traits will have done this for some time. It's best to tell him exactly what bothers you (not your opinion or interpretation of it), and that you understand it isn't something he does deliberately or because he's careless or lazy. If he accepts your observations and doesn't want to be doing the things that upset you but can't help it, then you can raise the issue of ADD. You may be relieved to find that he already knows something about it and has been thinking it over himself. In any case, give him time and space to digest what you're saying.

Whether you're in an established or a new relationship, you'll ultimately have to help your partner get professional help. Nonetheless, there are a number of things you can do to help him and your relationship before (and while) he's in treatment. Like your partner, you'll need to learn as much as you can about ADD, and try to understand what it explains about his behavior. Like him, try to direct as much of your anger about the ADD at the ADD, not at him or at yourself. Try to maintain as objective a perspective on his ADD as you can and, if possible, a sense of humor about the endlessly ludicrous and absurd events that ADD invariably precipitates. Above all, you'll need to avoid relationships with unbalanced roles and functions. These usually have a parent-child character, as we saw with the Satterlys. Unfortunately, someone with ADD has such a strong need to be taken care of that it's hard for him to avoid unbalanced relationships. Much of this book is concerned with preventing (or improving) alliances like these.

In either a new or established relationship, the next step is raising the question of professional help. If someone you're getting to know is willing to discuss this, and will consider getting help, you've probably got the beginnings of a good relationship. Or if the relationship has gone on for some time, his openness shows that it is on a solid footing. On the other hand, if he won't consider treatment, then you must decide if you can take him *as is*, because he isn't going to change. Be warned, though, that if this is a new relationship and he won't consider your feelings on the matter, then it's much less likely that a good relationship will develop. It *may* mean that in only this one area he's too sensitive, at least for now, to look at himself carefully, but that in all other areas he can be open, caring, and loving—and may, after a time, take care of his ADD. But you won't know that for a while, and you'll need to brace yourself for disappointment if his resistance is simply one example of a general unwillingness to deal with any serious topic with you.

Big Question #3: Can I Take Him As Is

As Satterly's various liaisons can tell you, not all cases of ADD are packaged unattractively. There are a number of very appealing and competent men and women with ADD. They've managed to find themselves a career niche, and have peopled or otherwise organized their lives in ways that work for them. I know a number of scientists and businessmen with serious attentional deficits who are nonetheless highly successful—their lives are brilliantly organized by an adoring supporting cast of spouse, friends, colleagues, and/or students. None would consider treatment for their ADD, and they probably never will.

Living with a person with ADD, even an accomplished one, is something of an art form, and you'll need some preparation if you decide to do it. Think about the list of questions you (or he) answered yes to, and make sure you understand that these things won't change. If he can't balance his checkbook or be gotten out of bed without dynamite, if he gets lost on the way to the mailbox, or if he can't understand why you (or anyone else) won't instantaneously do his bidding, then you'd better get used to it, because, without treatment, he'll be this way for the next ten decades. And there's no guarantee that treatment will change any of this even if he does agree to it. You, or someone you hire, will have to do all the things he can't. You'll also have to tolerate (and run interference for) his impulsiveness, organize his details, and learn to spot when he's drifting off—and then stop, ask, recap, and so on in order to communicate with him. If he's one of the very few successful ones, you'll have to put up with (and orchestrate and compensate) his supporting entourage. At the same time you'll be called submissive, regressive, codependent, and June Cleaver-esque. The experience and the critiques are a lot like those parents encounter when raising a child, except that this child won't grow up—especially without treatment.

On the other hand, many of us love child-rearing, and many people love being with an ADD partner. He's intelligent, always in motion, and (if anything) spontaneous. Still, be warned that even though the ADD doesn't change, *you* will change over the years. We're not programmed, after all, to raise children, let alone partners, forever. Over the years your own needs will change and develop, and if the burden of organizing your ADD partner keeps you from exploring and experiencing these changes, you'll very likely feel cheated. Marion Satterly went through this, and it ended her marriage.

Marion also felt the pressure of raising a child with a partner who has ADD. Few Wendell Satterlys have the patience and ongoing presence of mind to carry their share of the hard labor involved in child-rearing. Children's needs come first, and many a marriage, like the Satterlys', falls apart over the conflict of interest between children and spouse. It's even worse when ADD problems emerge in the children. This worsens the burdens of child-rearing, and, try as you might, it's impossible not to resent your partner (even if only subconsciously) for contributing, genetically, to something as troublesome to your child as ADD—especially during those times when he's *not* contributing practically to the child's care and control.

* * *

There are many other things to consider about a relationship with a person with ADD, but I've given you the main idea: Enter it with your eyes wide open. Study him, study the condition—and if the balance goes in his favor, do your best. Many people would find Ward or June Cleaver boring, and would rather marry a Klingon than live with one of those mellow, imperturbable icons of the fifties. Now that I think of it, that's not a bad metaphor—life with a Klingon can be a pretty good approximation of one with a human with ADD, and that can be very exciting.

But there will be moments . . .

CHAPTER 3

Mood Disorders and Their Effect on Relationships

As disruptive as ADD can be to a relationship, depression and mania can be even more trouble. Identifying them in oneself or in a partner can be especially difficult. Many people with depression are not aware of it, and those with mania are almost by definition completely unaware of it. As we saw in the last chapter, this is also true with ADD—but when a person learns he has ADD, he's likely to accept the diagnosis, may be greatly relieved, and quite often seeks and accepts help. In many cases of depression, and absolutely every case of mania, however, a person will deny his condition—often with a conviction that borders on delusional, and sometimes with a conviction that *is* delusional. This interferes with a partner's ability to recognize the condition as well, and therefore makes it less likely that he can do much about it.

Another factor making mood disorders troublesome to relationships is their intimate connection to interpersonal issues. Bouts of depression, for example, are most often precipitated by the loss of an important person, or by disappointments in others or in oneself—as in Mrs. Balusteri's depression following her infidelity. Manic episodes can be precipitated by the same factors.

Children who lose parents early are at higher risks for depression later in life. On the other hand, the security of a good relationship and a satisfying social life diminishes the likelihood of a depressive episode.

We'll begin with the downside of the mood disorder spectrum—depression and its lesser variant, dysthymia.

Depression

Everyone knows the feeling of depression: a sense of sadness or disappointment, often with feelings of loneliness, emptiness, or guilt, usually experienced in the context of loss, disappointment, or disillusionment. In most circumstances, these feelings are of mild or moderate intensity, and dissipate quickly enough not to be significantly disruptive. As we saw in Chapter One, however, for people prone to mood disorders, they can become intense and persistent enough to develop into full medical syndromes. Jennine Balusteri's chagrin and embarrassment over her infidelity quickly escalated into a frenzy of self-recrimination, unrelenting agitation, and an escalating despair that led her to the brink of suicide. Only her religious convictions and her husband's timely intervention prevented this catastrophe.

Jennine's condition was an unfortunately good example of a depressive episode as defined by the APA's DSM-IV, the latest edition, published in 1994. If untreated, such an episode can last up to a year or more, though the average duration is around six months. There is usually a preliminary period of a few weeks to a few months during which the feelings of depression gradually escalate—though when the precipitants are sudden or of major proportions, the onset can be almost instantaneous, like Jennine's. Sometimes the factors are easy to determine, like the loss of a job or of a relationship; at other times the depression seems to come "out of the blue."

According to the DSM-IV criteria, a depressive episode usually includes:

1. A drop of mood along with a loss of interest in things that were previously compelling or important

2. Abnormalities of appetite and sleep (too much or too little of either)

3. An agitated restlessness or a paralysis of activity that can reach the point of stupor

4. Substantial anxiety, sometimes intense enough to mask the depressive aspects of the disorder

5. Difficulty in thinking, concentrating, or remembering, all of which cause major difficulties at work

6. Loss of contact with reality—the patient may hear voices, see visions, or develop delusional ideas.

7. Delusions of persecution, infidelity, or of bizarre physical deterioration (rotting intestines, insect-infested brain, and so on) can occur

8. Preoccupation with thoughts of death and suicide. One of six patients with a major depressive disorder will eventually commit suicide.

Some forms of depression are chronic rather than episodic. Even before her major depressive episode, Mrs. B. suffered from a chronic state of low self-esteem and shyness, along with intermittent but extended periods of despondency, pessimism, and helplessness. DSM-IV defines this state of chronic mild to moderately severe depression dysthymia, a very common condition despite the fact that its prevalence has been vastly underestimated until recently. (For years psychiatrists assumed that any chronic depressive condition had a purely psychological basis, even though there was no data whatever to substantiate this. Research shows, in fact, that dysthymia has a clear biological basis, and that it responds as well to medication as does a major depressive episode.) When a depressive episode becomes superimposed on a background of chronic dysthymia, it is called double depression. This occurs at least once in about twenty-five percent of dysthymics.

Jennine Balusteri's condition, then, is a textbook case of double depression and, like most textbook cases, isn't very common. Most cases (like Mr. B., for example) don't fit tidy descriptions, and thus many of them go unrecognized. They often involve a few, sometimes only one, of the symptoms. Often they're a collection of depressive character traits (like irritability or sullenness), and tend to fool medical and nonmedical therapists alike.

About one in five people will suffer a depression sometime during his life; it's not so easy to list guidelines for understanding or identifying such a large and diverse population. One complicating factor is that the depression is influenced, sometimes very strongly, by the personality it affects. Thus in the case of a mild depression in a person with a strong personality, there may be little or no sign of the depression. Nonetheless, from time to time the depression may assert itself—in angry outbursts or bouts of crying or drinking. If the personality is strong enough, the outward signs of even a serious depression can be suppressed. Here I have in mind people like Abraham Lincoln or Winston Churchill, each of whom suffered from serious depressive disorders but rose above them to prevail through supremely trying times.

In similar fashion, creative people can channel their depressive experience into productivity. Suffering as they do, they see more deeply into the darker aspects of life, and struggle to understand, in philosophical, spiritual, or artistic terms, why life contains so much suffering, injustice, and tragedy. One thinks of Edgar Allan Poe, through the weary midnight hours mourning a lost love—and making something beautiful, a poem, from something unbearable, the grief of his irreplaceable loss. How the people I'm describing can contain their suffering, or channel it into creativity, while others cannot (thereby allowing their depressive feelings to disrupt their interpersonal relationships) is an intriguing question. Whether they have a greater tolerance for mental pain, or a more complex psychological makeup that allows them to contain their suffering within themselves, is also intriguing—but we don't have to answer these questions here. For the moment, we'll stay with the practical.

As I said, some people can't contain their depressive feelings very well, and therefore spread their misery to others. For convenience, we can divide the people I'm describing into three groups: the sad and lonely depressives, the guilty and perfectionistic depressives, and the angry and sullen depressives. These categories will be useful later in discussing the interpersonal effects of different types of depression. In practice, of course, the groups shade into one another.

The guilty and perfectionistic depressive is overly self-critical and irrationally guilt-ridden. He is preoccupied with his failures and inadequacy—that is, in most cases, not reaching an unreasonably high goal or not mastering an unrealistically difficult assignment. He is relentlessly demanding of himself and absolutely inconsolable about his inadequacies. He usually holds unreasonably high standards for others as well as for himself, and can be severely critical if they don't meet these standards. If, on the other hand, he keeps his criticism entirely to himself, its full force can sink him into a dejected state of remorse and regret, effectively isolating him from those around him. Either way, he is distressing to people trying to be close to him.

His personality when he's depressed is simply an exaggeration of how it is during normal times, that is, even at his best he's perfectionistic and fastidious toward himself and others, and feels (and often acts) condescending toward anyone without his demonic drive for perfection. People like this are difficult—especially if you're in a relationship with one. It hurts, after all, if your partner doesn't feel you're good enough. It tends to make you feel resentful, sometimes to the point of giving up altogether on trying to please him. Or, what's worse, if you're something of a guilty depressive yourself, you're likely to grind yourself into dust trying to meet his ever-escalating demands.

The sad and lonely depressive is typically preoccupied with the loss of a beloved person, a job, or other circumstance that had formerly provided emotional support or status. He's obsessed with longing for reunion with whomever or whatever was lost. He's sad and tearful, often whiny, clingy, and inconsolable in his demands for comfort and support. Even when not overtly depressed, his exaggerated sensitivity to even a hint of rejection makes him demand continuous companionship and acceptance—all in the face of a behavior style guaranteed to push away all but those most devoted to him. His demands are all the more exasperating since, unlike those of the guilty or angry depressive, they're usually expressed only indirectly, by inference, allowing him to deny his insatiability if confronted. All this is terribly disruptive of relationships, but can also lead to a stable, if problematic, attachment to a person, who, for his or her own reasons, feels compelled to spend much of her life satisfying her partner's imperious but unstated demands.

The third type, the angry, sullen depressive, can be the most difficult to identify. George Balusteri is a good example. At its worst, the style combines the most annoying traits of the other two. Here the hypercriticism of the guilty depressive and the litany of lament of the lonely depressive are turned outward at whatever target is at hand. No one and no thing satisfy him, and he's filled with indignation at anyone who doesn't fulfil his whims or wishes to the letter—whether he's stated them or not. At the same time, the mildest rejection or censure of him precipitates a torrent of indignation and complaints of abuse and neglect. People are either intimidated or driven away by this behavior. Sometimes a partner shares the feeling that the angry depressive does deserve unconditional nurturance and support, and, in an ongoing frenzy of masochism and compliance, devotes his or her life to providing them. Jennine Balusteri endured this posture for decades. The fact that on the surface the sullen depressive doesn't seem to be depressed obscures the dynamics of the relationship, making it all the more of a trap. The compliant partner often becomes progressively miserable and, ultimately, depressed—because a partner who allows this is usually prone to depression himself. As with the Balusteris, the pattern can be stable for decades.

As I said, the psychological factors perpetuating a bad relationship with someone like George can be hidden. As a partner, what you don't know in a circumstance like this can certainly hurt you. It isn't easy to see, for example, that his sullen demands and endless complaints have almost nothing to do with you—they arise almost entirely from his depression. Before offering practical guidelines for avoiding (or getting out of) the traps depression can set for couples, I'll discuss the other pole of the mood disorders—mania.

Mania

Mania and its milder variants are less common than depression, but are so destructive that they deserve equal time here. They very often fuel the sorts of betrayal and infidelity that routinely ruin relationships. Even without overt abandonment or infidelity, the personality style of people susceptible to manic disorders leads to chronic abuse and neglect that over time can erode the best of relationships.

Mania is the upper pole, so to speak, of the bipolar disorders, the second major class of mood disorders. Bipolar disorder involves a series of manic and depressive episodes throughout life, with periods of normal mood and functioning in the time separating the episodes. Manic episodes are shorter than those of depression, typically lasting a few weeks, and usually begin and end more abruptly. The symptoms are the polar opposite of those in a depressive episode:

1. inflated mood with grandiosity or irritability
2. excessive sexual interest and indiscretion
3. push to start but never finish a rash of projects simultaneously
4. reduced sleep
5. excessive talkativeness
6. a mad rush of ideas
7. increased distractibility

All these are accompanied by an often superhuman level of physical activity leading to impractical buying sprees, impulsive love affairs, foolish investments, and similarly ill-advised and disruptive activities.

A manic episode, once witnessed, is never forgotten. A typical example was Jane Worley, a thirty-year-old investment banker who was hospitalized for a depressive episode that had been going on for some two months. She had been withdrawn, tearful, and increasingly delusional; she felt that she was so evil and so worthless that God had arranged her hospitalization to protect his other, more worthy followers. She expressed this in a sad whisper on her first hospital day, and never repeated it.

On her seventh or eighth hospital day, she awoke with a start, let out a shriek like a banshee, and began bounding around the ward, spinning wildly and crashing violently into anyone in her path (a psychotic mechanical engineer nearby noted "the girl has significant rotational velocity"). For the first few orbits she was silent, but soon started to accompany her gyrations with an outpouring of jokes and puns at a rate that was barely believable. Each time she'd bounce off someone, she'd change the subject of her joking to whatever she'd gleaned of her victim. Bumping into a girl with a yellow dress, for example, she started joking and punning about bananas, lemons, and other incarnations of the color yellow. Her capacity was astonishing; one of the staff maintains to this day that she told fifty banana jokes in the space of one minute. Over the course of a few minutes her velocity (rotational and linear) increased to the point that she had to be restrained before she hurt herself or someone else. In the past, manics would literally exercise themselves to death in such wild states of excitement. After restraining her, we were all at a loss for words, though Sam, the schizophrenic engineer, announced casually that "Lady Jane seems different today."

With medication, individual therapy, and group therapy Jane's mania de-escalated over ten or twelve days, allowing a more leisurely view of what was happening in her mind. Most of the time her attention was a feather in the wind in any group of patients or staff discussing a number of topics at once—her attention and conversation jumping from one subgroup to another. All the while her conversation had a grandiose and theatrical component—she blurted out opinions and observations in grandly omniscient fashion without regard for whether anyone was attuned to what she was saying. It was as if she were onstage in front of a faceless audience about whom she had no concern other than how much she impressed them. It was also striking that all throughout her manic episode she had no idea whatever that there was anything wrong with her. She felt that spinning madly around the room was an expression of healthy exuberance, and that the victims of her "significant rotational velocity" were simply too slow or unimaginative to get out of her way, and therefore weren't worthy of concern. She also felt that anyone who couldn't follow her jokes or disjointed conversation was simply dull-minded and therefore uninteresting to her. At one point she announced in stentorian tones that God himself had told her (and only her) that she was his special child, and had commanded her to dance for him, thereby reversing her original (whispered) message that he had singled her out as especially troublesome.

At its most severe, a bipolar disorder involves alternations of extreme depressive and manic episodes. There is, however, a range of milder conditions that are much more common than the major forms. These can be more disruptive because they are more subtle, begin more gradually, and are therefore more difficult to identify and treat appropriately. These forms are hypomania and cyclothymia.

Hypomania is a milder form of mania, not severe enough to lead to psychosis or to serious disruption of functioning. Usually it comes and goes in episodes, but there are unusual cases of chronic hypomania, usually when the condition is relatively mild. A hypomanic is like Jane Worley with the volume turned down and the focus turned up a bit—always in motion in several directions at once, remarkably productive (usually in bursts), talking fast, moving fast, working fast, witty and charismatic. The mood is usually unreasonably cheerful, though sometimes it's just as unreasonably irritable. Like Jane, hypomanics are always onstage, and have difficulty seeing people in any way other than as members of their audience. Their capacity for warmth and empathy is therefore limited, even with their partners or children. Cyclothymia is a condition of alternating dysthymic and hypomanic cycles, usually separated by periods of normal mood.

There are some valuable aspects to hypomania. Bipolar patients in general are intelligent and creative, often to the point of genius; many if not most of the history's greatest geniuses have been bipolar. Their rapid and multidimensional thinking, with its ability to synthesize topics that at first blush seem (to the rest of us) unrelated, lead to a recognition of unexpected interrelationships and therefore to profound insights and dazzlingly creative productions. Mark Twain, perhaps the most charismatic American yet born, is a perfect example of cyclothymia. He did have periods of profound depression—especially after the loss of his twenty-four-year-old daughter and, later, of his wife. His black moods, however, which he immortalized so hauntingly in his autobiography and letters, never lasted very long. Most of the time he was at worst mildly depressed or irrepressibly hypomanic. His mind never rested—whether writing, talking, daydreaming, or even night dreaming, he was always creating. His conversation (and, of course, his writing) overflowed with puns, wordplay, metaphors, jokes, insights, and ideas—all brilliant, all charming, and all tossed off with as little effort as the rest of us use to produce a simple declarative sentence about the weather.

All these traits make a hypomanic terribly attractive—at a distance. In many if not most cases, though, they're hard to live with. Their traits, as I said, represent muted versions of the overtly psychotic mental process of full-scale mania like Jane Worley's episode. For one thing, their moods aren't always so joyful, but they're still creatively irritable (and irritating) when their moods turn sour. For another thing, the performance never ends, and this precludes two-way communication. Further, there's usually a kind of Teflon-coated impermeability to their personalities. The degree to which they fail to be moved by other people's feelings, rights, or agendas can be chilling.

A consummate capacity for denying any problems in themselves is one of the hypomanic's most uncharming qualities. Typically, the histrionically self-centered, driven, philandering, irritable, and grandiose hypomanic can't understand why his partner is unhappy—and therefore blames her for whatever goes wrong. What's worse, he's prone to run away from his troubles—flight-taking is characteristic of hypomanics. Thus a hypomanic's partner is not only blamed for whatever goes wrong, but also left alone to clean up the consequences. All in all, the partner feels betrayed, abandoned, and foolish as she's maneuvered into a relationship by a consummately charming character, only to discover over time that she's been living with a completely unmanageable, flight-taking philanderer who not only trashes his partner's self-esteem and leaves her life in shambles, but also coolly blames her for it all and runs away without a second thought.

Chapters Five to Seven show some of the ways hypomanics

upend their relationships as completely as Lady Jane upended her ward mates.

Practical Lessons: Identifying Mood Disorders

As I said earlier, a person who's depressed is sometimes the last to know it—a fact that confuses his assessment of his condition, and that of anyone who listens to him about it. Manics, of course, never know they're manic.

Part of the confusion is how powerfully your mood affects your view of yourself and the world. In a low mood, the world and yourself are gloomy and hopeless—in an elated mood, both are wonderful. Thus a depressed person thinks his low opinion of himself is simply accurate self-assesment. A manic or hypomanic, on the other hand, thinks that he has no problems whatever. This makes trying to help a manic or depressive all the more difficult. If you try to talk to your partner about his depression, you're likely to meet not only resistance, but also bewilderment—and if you try to talk to your partner about his mania, you're likely to find that he's gone to Kansas (unless he lives there already).

To make matters worse, mood disorders are usually episodic or cyclic. Thus a person with different moods at different times feels completely different about himself (and about you) during those times, and is usually unaware of the contradiction. The effect of all this can be demoralizing to a partner who takes it personally when he's called worthless by a depressed partner or abandoned by a manic one. It's even more difficult when the changes in mood and judgment are gradual or subtle, because then they're harder to identify. Things don't go much better with chronic dysthymic or hypomanic states. The person who's always been depressed, like a fish who's always been in water, isn't likely to think he's submerged in a depression. He simply assumes he's inadequate—and isn't likely to seek personal or professional help for an attitude he's taken for granted for so long. You may as well ask the fish to think about swimming through air instead of water—the water's always been there and will always be there, and if you don't like it, get out of it.

* * *

Dealing with mood problems is complicated, especially within a relationship. I belabor it here because if you don't know about the complexities, the job can become completely impossible. The following sections offer some tools and practical guidelines for making the task a little more negotiable—including calling in professional help.

A. How to Identify a Mood Disorder in Yourself

Depression

Since the DSM-IV symptom lists were constructed to bring objectivity into the chore of identifying treatable syndromes, the one for depression is a good place to start:

1. Has your mood been especially gloomy or irritable lately, and have periods of these moods lasted longer than usual?

2. Have you lost interest in things that usually appeal to you—sex, hobbies, the NFL, chocolate?

3. Do you wake up at three A.M. each night, and not fall back to sleep?

4. Do you have trouble focusing your attention, so that work takes you much longer than usual and you do it more poorly?

5. Have you lost your appetite? Have you lost weight?

6. Do you feel a continuous dread about the future—a feeling of agitation and restlessness, as if something bad is about to happen but you don't know what it is?

7. Do you have trouble remembering the simplest things that ordinarily would come to mind with no effort?

8. Are you preoccupied, or even obsessed, with feelings of death or suicide?

9. Do you feel that none of this will ever get better? Do you feel that there's nothing you can do to improve any of it?

If most of your answers are yes, then you're almost certainly suffering a major depressive episode. Many people, however, show only a few, sometimes only one, symptom on the list—but their symptoms are just as treatable. The most common "single-symptom syndromes" in my experience are a pervasive feeling of fatigue and the experience of insomnia—usually in the form of waking and staying awake at three or four A.M.

Answering these questions sounds easier than it is. Since no one likes to think there's anything wrong with his mind, let alone his brain, there's a strong tendency to make rationalizations for each yes answer. Unlike people with ADD, who usually feel relieved when they find themselves on an ADD symptom list, depressives tend to con themselves out of the obvious conclusion that a majority of yes answers means they're likely to be depressed.

Many depressives feel that carrying a major psychiatric diagnosis is another in a series of indignities they've endured and they can't bear it. At the same time, they feel so worthless and hopeless that they can't imagine deserving, let alone getting, help for any condition they might discover. Thus a depressive either falls back on the conviction that he's just no good and deserves to feel miserable, or he rationalizes all the "yeses" and concludes that he's not depressed: "The cat wakes me up at three A.M," for example, "I'm forty years old now, so of course sex isn't interesting anymore," "Work is boring, so of course I can't concentrate on it," and so on down the list. Reading a symptom list with someone else can help you be more objective—another person won't share your hopelessness about treatment or your mortification about a psychiatric diagnosis, and can therefore be more objective.

There are a number of more subtle signs that help identify a depression. Generally speaking, they are the social, emotional, or vocational consequences of being depressed. Do you find, for example, that you're an underachiever—working well below the potential you established when you were younger (or not depressed)? Do you find yourself easily overwhelmed by tasks that others (or yourself in better times) seem to breeze through? Is there one time of day when you feel the worst? A daily variation such that you feel your worst at one time of day (usually morning) is a strong indicator of a biologically based depression. (George

Balusteri, you'll recall, experienced this pattern—he was gloomier and more irritable each morning, and almost mellow by evening. He and Mrs. B., however, rationalized this as the result of his winding down after a full day of grumping and erupting.) Do you feel frightened or preoccupied about being impoverished financially even though there's no actual financial shortage? Do you spend a good deal of time wondering "why me?" and can't imagine doing anything to change your circumstances? Do you find that you can't find the strength to say no to any request even if you know it will bring you trouble at a time you can least deal with it? Is making even the smallest decision an ordeal, and is this a change from your usual style? In my experience, the inability to make decisions is one of the most reliable of these signs.

Do you find that spending time alone has become intolerable, and that you constantly need someone around to keep from getting painfully lonely and even panicky? Or do you find yourself alone and dissatisfied much of the time—and blaming everyone else for it? Do you feel, for example, that no one cares about you "as they should," or that no one gives you enough of what you (feel you) need or deserve? If so, you have to ask yourself if a depression is making you so needy and the world seem so withholding. The sense (or, worse, the reality) that people are always being unkind to you also points to a depression. If you feel this way, you have to ask if you're acting out a depression by letting people take advantage of you. As we'll see in Chapters Five through Seven, self-defeating maneuvers like these are common—partly because the depressed person feels he deserves it, and partly because he needs an objective reason for the otherwise incomprehensible (and therefore bewildering) feelings of badness and pain.

Mania

No one at the height of a manic episode understands himself. The best you can do is to discover the fact in retrospect. Fortunately manic episodes are time-limited. Likewise, even with chronic hypomania or cyclothymia, there are periods of relatively normal moods during which you can step back, survey the rubble your manic behavior has left in its path, and try to understand what happened. After a period, then, of self-indulgent and self-destructive activity, you'll have to look back and ask if your otherwise unaccountable behavior was driven by mania. Did you, for example, find yourself unrealistically elated or irritable? Was your mind racing and your speech pressured? Did you sleep less? Did you have sex more often and spend more money? Were you interested in anyone and everything, and did you explore it all with a level of energy and intrusiveness far beyond your usual limits? Here too, there are people who have only a few of the symptoms but whose condition is as treatable and biologically grounded as that of one with the full spectrum of manic symptoms. Manics often have trouble recalling their episodes, so you may need to rely on the recollections of someone who watched you during the episode (if he'll still speak to you).

How to Identify a Mood Disorder in Your Partner

Depression

Here too the symptom list is the place to start. Beyond this, since depression is such a common experience, your common sense and years of experience should help. The appearance of someone who's depressed, for example, is usually unmistakable—unless he's able to hide it by sheer force of will. Does he look sad, guilty, or sullen? Are his eyes teary, his posture slumped, and his gait listless? Does his voice have a monotone singsong drone that wears you out just to have to listen to it—like sad old Eeyore the donkey in the Winnie-the-Pooh stories? Do you find yourself feeling discouraged or demoralized, or even fatigued, when you're with him? Sometimes there's a tar-babyish sort of stickiness to a depressive—you just can't pry him loose. This is the result of his inability to let go of anything or anyone, and of his difficulty being alone. Getting a depressive off the phone can be an ordeal of diplomacy. Does he have an uncanny ability to find the negative in anything you say to him or do for him? A depressive can find the tiniest flaw or hesitation in the grandest compliment or gesture—and become so preoccupied with it that he misses everything else.

You'll recognize these characteristics as manifestations of our three types of depressives who intrude their problems into the lives of others—in this case, yours. As I mentioned in the last section, sometimes there's an even more pernicious, if subliminal, effect—a depressive can make you feel like abusing him, or at least taking advantage of him. What's happening is almost always out of awareness for both parties, but this only makes the effect more pernicious. To act out his need for punishment, the depressive will so frustrate, annoy, or otherwise distress people that out of sheer exasperation they abuse him. Sometimes, for example, his "sticky" inability to let you out of a conversation does it. Or his inability to say no or to defend himself from intrusions (along with his desperate need to be liked) keeps him from setting limits on what he'll do for people. Thus, if a person, including your partner, is always your first choice when someone's schedule needs to be pushed around, he's probably depressed.

Mania

A manic or hypomanic looks like a depressive or dysthymic in reverse—the elated expression, the sprightly gait, the lilt in his voice, and twinkle in his eye. If the depressive is adagio, the manic is allegro. Likewise, his effect on you is the reverse of the depressive's—his enthusiasm is infectious and you risk becoming grandiose yourself and irrationally carried away with whatever manicky (or maniacal) scheme he may be delighting in at the moment (manics make great salesmen). Sometimes, though, the effect is just the opposite. The ever-intrusive manic has an uncanny ability to cut through your defenses, put his finger on your touchiest sensitivities, and manipulate you with them. He either caresses your points of pride to make you sympathetic to his schemes ("as someone shrewd enough to be in your position surely knows...") or, if he's so inclined, stomping on your vulnerabilities to punish or intimidate you into doing what he wants ("surely you're not still using a 386 machine?"). Manics are physically intrusive as well—standing too close, sometimes touching you too much, and otherwise not respecting conventional interpersonal boundaries. I find, for example, that if someone walks right past my waiting room, down the hallway, and into my office, a diagnosis of mania is all but certain.

Effects on Communication

As with ADD, the symptoms of depression or mania are especially disruptive in their effects on communication. A number of impasses typically occur in communication with a person with a mood disorder. Thus if you find yourself at one of these impasses with a partner, your exasperation may help identify a mood disorder in one or both of you—if you can stop to think about your predicament objectively. I'll try to describe the impasses so that both a person with a mood disorder and his partner can recognize them. It's much easier for a partner to spot them, but it's generally more useful when the mood-disordered partner catches on to one of them. He's the one, after all, who has to come to terms with his problems and then do something to bring them under control. This is more difficult with a mood disorder than with almost any other psychiatric disorder.

At their most extreme, both depression and mania shut down communication altogether. The depressive becomes mute, and the manic becomes so entangled in psychotic babble that nothing he says makes sense to anyone but himself (if that). Even in less severe cases (including dysthymia) a depressive's communication is hindered by his gloomy preoccupations. His relentless self-criticism can make any remark distressing. It's impossible, for example, to praise him—he'll think you're either foolish and misreading him, or else insincere and trying to manipulate him. Thus you're stuck in the exasperating impasse that everything you say is heard as critical, manipulative, or stupid—and, to add incrimination to injury, sooner or later it's all held against you. Typically, a partner will withdraw, get angry, or wear himself out insisting that he's not being critical—often to the point of becoming very critical of his partner's stubborn inability to communicate reasonably.

Conversation with a manic is also an exercise in exasperation but the details are different. The manic (and to a lesser degree, the hypomanic) is always onstage, and anyone in conversation with him is simply a member of his audience. He's much more concerned with making what he says charming, brilliant, or otherwise impressive than he is with adapting its content to what his listener can understand or learn from it. Any attempt to bring your own ideas into the conversation is treated as an interruption of the performance. Anyone who wants to communicate as an equal, or share a relationship between equals, eventually tires of the endless performance—and the relationship suffers from his disillusionment with what he initially imagined the manic had to offer.

Irritability inhibits communication with either a manic or depressive. You're strolling along in conversation and boom—you've stepped where you shouldn't, and he explodes in rage. From his point of view, of course, the explosions make psychological sense. They're responses to what, in his distorted perception, he thinks are put-downs. Over time a partner becomes fearful of stepping into any topic, and communication falters, usually along with the relationship.

What makes this communication mine field especially treacherous is that the mine field himself is so often unaware of how his outbursts affect his partner and their relationship. The manic, by the very nature of his disorder, rarely understands any effect of his behavior on others—including, of course, his outbursts. It's similar for an irritable hypomanic, but less exaggerated. The depressive or dysthymic all too often rationalizes his explosive hypersensitivity as a reasonable response to what he thinks are insults or attacks. Jennine Balusteri's pre-Prozac experience of her gloomy and explosive husband was an unfortunate example of this process.

If as a partner, then, you find yourself in a mine field like Mr. B.'s, or if your partner communicates in the theatrical or self-flagellating style of the manic or depressive, it is very useful to understand what underlies it all. For one thing, it removes any uncertainty you've had about his having a mood disorder. It can also help you be more tolerant of something he really can't control (without treatment). It's more difficult for the person with the mood disorder to recognize its effect on communication—but if he does recognize it, he's come a long way. Someone with a manageable degree of hypomania, for example, can, with a good deal of effort, allow a little give-and-take in communication. A person with a relatively mild depression may be able to get some perspective on how he turns any comment into criticism or ridicule, and over time come to feel differently about what's said to him. In most cases, though, it takes a course of treatment to correct them—by resolving the mania or depression that disrupts the communication in the first place.

Practical Lessons: What to Do and What Not to Do

As in the last chapter, I'll suggest some ways to help your partner deal with his mood disorder—both before you can get him to professional help, and as ways to support and facilitate what professionals can do for him. For both partners, education should be first and foremost. The more you know about the stereotypic symptoms and behavior traits of the conditions, the better. It's useful to know, for example, that what precipitates both mania and depression is usually a loss (of a person, a valued possession, or valued aspect of oneself). It's especially useful to know that specific things precipitate manic or depressive episodes for particular individuals. Alcohol and marijuana cause mania or depression in some individuals, for example; reduced sleep and overstimulating social events typically precipitate mania in others. Knowing about these triggers helps you keep alert for early signs of mania or depression, which can be very subtle and easy to miss. The following are a number of areas that are especially useful for you to know about.

Getting Perspective

Because mood so strongly affects how people think, it's terribly important (and terribly difficult) to maintain objectivity about what a depressed or manic person thinks, feels, or does. For a partner this means doing what you can not to take the depressive's criticism (or the manic's praise) literally. This is easier said than done. Consider, for example, a man I saw the other day, who had been happily married—at least, he thought so—for over twenty years. Suddenly his wife tells him that he has always been a spineless, unlovable bastard, details this in a hundred ways, and storms off to points unknown. It's hard not to take this personally. Nonetheless, if the change is really that sudden, in all likelihood it isn't personal. It's most likely that his wife has in fact been as happy as he's thought all along, but the precipitous onset of a serious depression has wiped out her good feelings and replaced them with misery and complaints. If he can get a toehold on this point of view, he can avoid retaliating in kind and risking a disruption of a viable relationship. He can then bear with her until her depression is treated (or otherwise remits)—at which point she too can look back and try to get some perspective on what's happened.

It's important to maintain emotional distance from the troublesome aspects of your partner's mood disorder. For depression, there are several traps to avoid. One is having your own moods controlled by those of your partner. The process can seem like a contagious disease, as a depressive inflicts his mood on others. You approach him in a perfectly good mood, but after a few minutes of listening to him talk about topics like the national debt or the crime rate, or how haggard and overworked you look, or how long he's been out of a job, you start to get down in the dumps. This is especially exasperating if he comes to feel better after depressing you. It's like handing over a hot potato (full of depression). The process, in other words, has reward value for him. People like this leave a trail of gloomy victims behind him, and sometimes this includes a trail of partners.

The depressive's irritability can also facilitate the process of his controlling your mood. What happens is that you become embroiled in tantrums and shouting matches without either of you learning much of what the other is saying or feeling. These angry interchanges can lead to an entanglement of emotions in which both of you become depressed, or more depressed. Sometimes it's guilt that gives a depressed partner control over the other. The depressive, for example, threatens suicide unless his partner complies with one of his wishes or agendas. Bold threats like "if you leave me, I'll kill myself," or more subtle ones like "if you don't want to spend more time here, I don't know what's left to live for," can keep a partner trapped in a relationship that's doing him no good whatever.

How can you avoid all this? For one thing, not playing along (not being provoked to anger or inappropriate caretaking, not responding to guilt-inducing maneuvers, and so on) helps your partner learn that his problems are within him, and aren't something that you do to him. Controlling yourself in the face of provocations—which escalate in intensity and stealth as they're ignored—is no easy task. Try to avoid counterattacking when he blames you for his troubles, or being blackmailed by his talk of suicide (this includes taking his threats at face value and calling in professional help). Try to talk to him without accusation. Avoiding blaming each other keeps you out of outlandish and endless debates in order to establish once and for all who's responsible for the misery in the relationship—as if this were possible (or would be useful if it were possible).

One time-tested way to do this is by speaking in the first person (using "I" messages rather than "you" messages). A depressed person will respond much better to the statement "I feel terribly sad, and frightened, when you talk about drinking yourself to death," than to "You upset me when you drink so much and talk like you do." All this is easier if you keep in mind that the depression is the ultimate villain—not you or your partner. Staying unencumbered by your partner's depression is much easier if you develop your own life, independent of dealing with his depression. This involves things like getting your attention back on work or school, keeping up hobbies, seeing friends, doing volunteer work, and so on.

For mania, getting perspective is no easier. It's hard not to take it personally when your partner blindsides you by running off, diving into a dozen publicly humiliating affairs, and losing your life savings in a flurry of disastrous business ventures. To the extent that you can remember that the real villain is the mania, the better are your chances of getting your partner, yourself, and your relationship the right sort of help.

Maintaining emotional distance can be a major problem for the partner of someone prone to mania. It is easy to get caught up in the grandiosity of a manic, for example. As he presents his complex schemes for riches and fame, he has an uncanny capacity to hoodwink you into colluding with his (unstated, and therefore all the more convincing) conviction that you and he are the only two people clever enough to understand (and pull off) the whole series of implausibilities. The feeling he gives you is one of being "bigger than life"—and it is very seductive. If you don't watch yourself, especially if you've just met your manic, this feeling can be very gratifying—for a while. If you're in a relationship with someone prone to hypomania or mania, you've got to keep alert to the danger sign that this feeling represents, and react accordingly.

The hard part, of course, is knowing what's involved in "reacting accordingly." The best way to deal with a manic episode, of course, is to prevent it—for example, by keeping an eye on your partner when he's sleep-deprived or becoming overstimulated, and then trying to get him to sleep and away from all the stimulation. Try to recognize his specific triggers for manicky periods, and do what you can to help him avoid them. By the very nature of his disorder, a mania-prone individual will deny that there's anything wrong with him, even as his mood approaches the stratosphere. One approach in putting the brakes on a manic or hypomanic episode is, rather than labeling the person's behavior and thought as problematic, describing them in ways more palatable to him—but true nonetheless. Especially useful, I've found, is something like "I don't think you understand your effect on other people." This gratifies his sense of power and specialness so that he can look at himself and his behavior a little more objectively.

Another approach is expressing common sense and simple truths about the person's condition. Usually it's as ineffective as any attempt to present mundane reality to this grand master of denial, but it's also harmless, and occasionally works wonders—so it's worth a try. For example, back in college a friend was slipping into what hindsight tells me was at least a hypomanic episode. He explained (at great length) to anyone who'd listen his special position in the mind of God (I can't recall the details, but do recall a grand intricacy and eccentricity in his convictions). I was completely bewildered by it all, and could say only something like "Do you really believe any of that?" To my surprise, he thought it over, decided "No, I guess not," shrugged his shoulders, and walked away. As far as I could tell, he seemed as normal as any other college senior for the rest of the time I knew him. Clearly, this is an unusually grand effect of such a simple remark (that's why I remember it after thirty years), but it's not altogether unrepresentative of the effect of the truth simply stated to someone escalating into mania. It can be a grand relief to not be taken seriously about a conviction like being God's favorite or even God himself (convictions that, deep down, these people know are not true). I suspect this had a lot to do with the good effect of what I'd said to my friend.

As we go along, I'll set up some concrete guidelines for being able to hang on and then get professional help in circumstances like these, especially in Chapter Ten. The perspective I'm suggesting, by the way, is something that counselors, mediators, divorce attorneys, judges, and others who deal with family issues need to attain—so that they can avoid facilitating separation or divorce in circumstances in which they should be facilitating treatment instead.

Limiting the Damage: A Fundamental Rule

The better a person functions, the better he feels. In this way, mood is a sort of built-in motivational consultant—we reward ourselves by feeling good whenever we do something well, and punish ourselves by feeling bad whenever we do something badly, or don't do it at all. Thus whenever a mental disorder limits how well a person functions, his mood drops. When the problem is a depression, mood can plunge especially precipitously.

Because of this, a very important rule is that if your depression makes you feel like giving up on doing something, important or not, you should try your best to do it anyway. If waking up at three A.M. makes you want to call in sick, for example, do your best not to. Better to struggle through a day's work than to stay at home, sinking deeper and deeper into depression, all the while calling yourself weak-willed and wimpy for staying home. If your depressed partner says he simply can't find the energy to do something he's always done, try to get him to do what he can, and, unless the consequences of not doing it are drastic, don't do it for him. The worst thing you can do is to patronize a depressed partner by taking over for him. On the other hand, you don't want to demoralize him by pushing him past his capacity, diminished as it is by his depression. Thus you'll need to walk a fine line between babying and bullying—your partner's doctor should help you with this. See Chapters Five through Seven and Chapter Eleven for guidelines and practical suggestions.

Taking Suicidal Talk (or Action) Seriously

The old chestnut that "anyone who talks about suicide won't do it" is completely false and therefore extremely dangerous. The majority of people who die by their own hand have in fact told someone about their intention—usually repeatedly. The fact that one out of every six people with a depressive disorder eventually die by suicide shows how ill-advised it is not to take suicidal feelings in yourself or suicidal talk in a partner absolutely seriously. If you find yourself feeling this way, get help. If your partner talks about suicide, get him help. People worry that they're being manipulated and will look foolish if they respond to a partner's threats of suicide, but remember, once you miss the chance to prevent a suicide, you don't get a second chance. You'll get over looking foolish. Besides, even if a person is trying to manipulate you, taking him seriously and bringing him for help allows a therapist to help both of you get past whatever issues are being played out with such a destructive game.

It's easy to forget that the suicide risk is also significant for manics. Manics may be elated and expansive, and their grandiosity can reach such proportions that it shades into the conviction of invulnerability. I knew a young man who boasted that he was so invulnerable that he could drive his car right through solid concrete walls—and died trying to do so at 100 miles per hour. Thus if a manic says something that has the potential to cause himself great harm (or death), take it very seriously and get professional help.

Getting Someone Past His Resistance to Getting Help

A number of attitudes that routinely prevent a depressed person getting treatment are themselves symptoms of the depression. The conviction, for example, that "I should be able to pull out of this myself" can sound like healthy pride asserting itself, but it usually covers a deeper and more problematic conviction like "I'm too worthless to deserve anyone's help." At other times, depressed people reject help with the lament "there's no one who can help me"—an attitude that can immobilize those around him, especially if they don't have much respect for the mental health profession. You have to understand that the lament is not a cynical (or shrewd) assessment of an ineffectual profession—it's an expression of the despair and hopelessness that are part of every serious depression.

Likewise, it's important to keep in mind that the manic will invariably discount the seriousness of his mental problems. Thus, paying attention to what he does (philander, speak with great speed and pressure, start a million projects and then abandon them) rather than what he says allows a clearer view of his mental difficulties. Nonetheless, it's hard to get him to professional help. Sometimes the approach suggested earlier helps: "You don't understand your effect on people." That is, you can sell the idea of treatment as a way to understand this aspect of his problem—and, as far as it goes, it's a true statement.

Male-Female Issues

I may have given the impression so far that men and women experience the various psychiatric syndromes in the same ways. This is not true, and I hope the examples throughout the book will make some of the differences clear. For the moment, I'll mention just two issues.

The first is premenstrual syndrome (PMS). However controversial this disorder remains (is it, some people wonder, really a disorder?), a few things about it are certain—that it has a biological basis and that it brings a period of depression or irritability (or both) to a great many women. In my experience, many women feel just as depressed several days each cycle as they would in the middle of a major depressive episode. And all the relationship problems I've mentioned here apply during those days. Their partners (male or female) tell me about this continually. Thus what I've said here and throughout the book about mood disorders can help to deal with PMS.

The second issue is just as commonplace. Men tend to be better doers than they are listeners, and this does help in some contexts, but not when they're trying to help someone who's depressed. It's rare to talk to a depressed woman who doesn't wish the men in her life would listen to her more and try to "fix" her less. Too many of us men seem to worry that women complain too much about how they feel, and that it's best not to indulge this sort of thing. In truth, women (and men) in emotional pain need to be heard, understood, and cared about, not fixed or lectured to, especially with something as difficult to fix as depression (without training and an armamentarium of treatment). Having you hear, understand, and simply stay with them can bring tremendous relief to people who are depressed. It always amazes the men how good they feel themselves when they put aside the handyman approach and simply listen and share the experience.

Avoiding Listening to and Giving Bad Advice

Nowhere is bad advice more dangerous than with the mood disorders. This is partly because a depressive, with his pervasive sense of worthlessness, is unlikely to defend himself from the nonsense people insist on preaching to him—and partly because the stakes are so high. Manics, on the other hand, never listen to anything—which in this one context may be a virtue. It's impossible to list all the bad advice depressives have to endure, but here are a few representative items. I list them to caution depressed people not to heed them and their partners not to preach them.

"Just buck up."
This shows him that you don't understand him and his experience—and makes him feel, in his exaggerated gloominess, that you probably will never be emotionally available to him.

"You just need to try harder."
Like "Just buck up," this shows a lack of understanding and makes him feel guilty for not trying hard enough.

"Anyone in your circumstances would be depressed."
This shows a disregard for his unique feelings about his circumstances—which are different from anyone else's.

"You'll need to get to the psychological roots of your problems before you can get better."

This isn't true for anyone seriously depressed. What's worse, the comment deepens his depression because it tells him that relief can come only through the onerous task of rooting out the psychological basis of his symptoms—something he knows he can't do.

"You're just looking for attention."

This comment is especially pernicious. It betrays that you're feeling angry and frustrated with him. No depressive will miss this, and will feel (correctly) that you're not there for him anymore.

"You're enjoying your depression and the power it gives you."

This comment is as dangerous as the preceding two. It drips with the poison of presuming that you can read the depressive's mind. Nothing good can come from this. If he doesn't feel you can read him accurately, he'll feel betrayed; if he does feel you can read him accurately, he's left with the unsettling sense that all his faults are visible to anyone who looks at him. In my experience, most attempts to tell a depressive what you think his actions "really" mean are delivered in anger and are self-protective. Comments like "You're enjoying staying in bed all day, aren't you?" or "You're in bed all day just to make me work harder to pay the bills" are inaccurate, guilt-producing, and may push the depressive closer to suicide.

But, you'll ask, what do you say? I don't have a good answer, except that the less you try to say, the better. You have to remember that a person in a serious depression feels a deep sense of loss. We saw in Chapter One that the physiological basis of depression is linked to the feelings of mother and child during separation. Thus a useful guideline is to imagine what you could say to console a child whose mother has just left, even momentarily. You can't say anything. No word, no act can penetrate the sadness. You can only offer, by silent gesture, to hold the child and let him cry. As we've seen, almost nothing you can say will penetrate a depressive's shroud of misery—at best, you can accept and reflect his feelings. Thus, if it's your partner, usually the most useful thing you can do is to simply hold him—both literally and figuratively. Being able to cry, being heard and understood in the arms of someone he loves and trusts, can be a great comfort.

We'll leave the discussion of mood disorders now and turn to a set of disorders in which the experience of anxiety is the central component.

CHAPTER 4

ANXIETY DISORDERS AND THEIR EFFECT ON RELATIONSHIPS

Like "depression," the term "anxiety" means different things to different people, and for any one person the experience can take different forms at different times. Like depression, anxiety is universal. At its mildest, it's a vague awareness that something as yet unknown is threatening one's well-being. If the threat does become known, the experience of anxiety shades into that of fear. As you reach a state of intense anxiety, you feel shaky and irritable, sometimes light-headed, your hands get cold and clammy, you feel a lump in your throat, break out in a cold sweat, and lose your ability to concentrate or think straight. If it goes on long enough, you may have trouble sleeping, feel fatigued, or experience abdominal distress or diarrhea. At its most extreme, anxiety reaches the level of panic—an overwhelming sense of terror, accompanied by physical symptoms like crushing chest pain or difficulty breathing, along with feelings of being completely out of control of your body or your mind.

Mild anxiety, on the other hand, is not only normal, it's useful—and sometimes indispensable. It's the way your brain lets you know that there may be trouble afoot—so you'd better stop, look around, and think things over. Some years back I was hiking in Yosemite, when a chipmunk on a tree stump a few feet ahead caught my eye. Ordinarily his sitting so close and so still would have delighted me—but not this time. For no reason I could imagine, I became anxious and unable to keep walking. The chipmunk, it finally occurred to me, was sitting altogether too still, and for too long—so I looked around and learned something useful: It was the mesmerizing effect of a four-foot-long rattlesnake that had the chipmunk sitting so still.

My brain, all this is to say, didn't trust my conscious mind to think through the circumstance without some physiological help. Recognizing that things are amiss when a chipmunk sits so still so close to a person, it stopped me in my tracks with the sudden production of anxiety. Without this signal, I'm sure my mind would have convinced itself that the little guy was sitting so still because he'd been tamed by years of cookies and nuts, and let me risk an ill-advised encounter with the slithery hypnotist. The adventure, then, is a pedestrian example of Freud's conception of signal anxiety: an internal signal sent to your conscious mind that something is wrong. Freud contrasted this with panic anxiety: anxiety of such intensity that it completely immobilizes functioning. A person I know, for example, walked over to admire a swimming pool at a house he was visiting and saw his five-year-old son lying at the bottom of the water. Up to that moment he hadn't known the boy was anywhere near the pool. The absolute unexpectedness and terrifying implications of what he saw raised his anxiety to a panic of such proportions that he couldn't move (mercifully, a twelve-year-old standing nearby saw the father's agitation, investigated, and rescued the boy before he suffered any neurological damage).

Anxiety of such overwhelming intensity cannot be explained in purely psychological terms. No degree of mental conflict about his child, for example, could immobilize the father so completely. Rather, it was the maladaptive overactivation of his brain's emergency (flight-or-fight) system that transformed his mental function into a chaos of undirected activity, leaving his brain incapable of initiating appropriate action.

In the last chapter I said that mood disorders are intimately related to interpersonal experiences (the precipitation of depression by the loss of a partner, the infectious nature of mania, and so on), and that because of this they're particularly hard on relationships. There are intrinsic interpersonal components to anxiety as well (anxious responses to a partner's absence, the escalation of anxiety when two anxious people interact, and the like). More commonly, however, anxiety tends to focus a person's attention on his own issues and away from other people—except for what they've done (if anything) to trigger the anxiety.

Thus the anxiety disorders can pull people away from relationships altogether or else push them toward relationships distorted by the special needs created by their anxiety (themes elaborated in Chapters Five and Six). In the following sections I'll present enough about these disorders to prepare us for discussion of the relationship problems they cause.

The Details of Anxiety: Seven Disorders

Any psychiatric disorder can generate anxiety, but the so-called anxiety disorders are a group for which anxiety is the central feature. DSM-IV defines a number of these disorders of which seven will be important to us. These are specific phobia, social phobia, agoraphobia, generalized anxiety disorder (GAD), panic disorder, obsessive-compulsive disorder (OCD), and post-traumatic stress disorder (PTSD).

Anxiety disorders are very common, though most people aren't at all familiar with them. Social phobia, for example, is present in thirteen percent of the general population, and OCD in around two percent. The disorders, therefore, affect millions of people, many if not most of whom think they're the only ones to suffer in the ways they do. And since the disorders are treatable, you can literally save a person's interpersonal life by helping him identify, accept, and then get treatment for one of them.

If you don't know something about the disorders, you're likely to mistake their symptoms for unpleasant personality traits—the symptoms of OCD, say, for stubbornness, or those of a phobia for timidity. Thus you can completely misunderstand anyone suffering from one of these conditions, and lose the chance to help him find treatment. If it's your partner (or a potential partner), you'll risk responding to his symptoms in all the wrong ways, thereby courting a range of disasters from getting trapped in a dismal relationship to upending a potentially good one. Many people react to OCD rituals, for example, with irritation and scolding, or to phobias with nagging, lecturing, and other promptings into circumstances the phobics can't handle—and at best demean and at worse deepen their partners' sufferings. If, on the other hand, you suffer from one of the disorders yourself and don't know it, you're at risk for all these problems plus the likelihood of having trouble getting into a relationship in the first place (this is discussed in Chapter Seven). And if that's not enough, people who don't understand their conditions are at risk for pursuing expensive, time-consuming, and often ineffective types of treatment—"adding invoice to injury," as a patient once called this enterprise.

Specific Phobia (Formerly, Simple Phobia)

Phobias are intense fears of specific objects or situations. They persist despite a person's knowing they're excessive or unreasonable. They're classified as anxiety disorders because anxiety is generated when a person encounters something he fears, or even anticipates encountering it. The fears often involve being hurt by the feared object (hit by a vehicle, bitten by a dog, killed in a plane crash); other times they involve the fear of losing control, panicking, or fainting in the presence of a frightening situation (the sight of blood, heights, closed-in spaces). Sometimes the anxiety reaches the point of a full-scale panic attack. Phobias are common in childhood, affecting up to twenty-five percent of children, but in most cases they fade away before adolescence.

If a phobia is mild, or limited to something you can avoid, you may suffer little disruption of your life. On the other hand, if the phobias are intense or unavoidable, your vocational and personal life can be seriously constricted. Fears of air travel, big cities, or crowded rooms, for example, can limit job performance and advancement. Likewise, fear of crowds or closed-in places restrict social life because these situations are hard to avoid early in a relationship.

An important interpersonal problem for a phobic is that he's likely to choose a partner with a hidden psychological agenda requiring a phobic person in his life. Some people, for example, are very fearful (or phobic) themselves, and deal with their feelings of humiliation about this by choosing a partner to whom they can feel superior. Others, for a variety of reasons, have a strong need to control. A phobic is so terrified of his phobic object that he's easily manipulated and controlled by someone who purports to protect him from it—and is therefore easy prey for someone with a need to control him.

Social Phobia

Social phobics are people who seem shy and standoffish. Until you know better, it's easy to think of them as inhibited or impaired because of a history of trauma or of ongoing psychological conflicts. Instead, research and clinical experience is teaching us that social phobics have specific biologically determined vulnerabilities. By definition the disorder involves interpersonal discomfort and therefore leads to significant limitations in social life. It involves a strong and persistent fear of either a specific social circumstance (like speaking in public, using a public rest room) or of social situations generally. The person's main concern is being embarrassed in the feared situation. He fears that others will find him anxious, foolish, crazy, or stupid—and that this will leave him feeling humiliated. People afraid of speaking in public, for example, fear that others will hear their voices waver, see their hands shake, or find them inarticulate. Most simply avoid the social situation they fear.

In the feared situation social phobics almost always have physical symptoms of anxiety (palpitations, trembling, sweating, abdominal distress, blushing, diarrhea, confusion). They also experience a significant degree of anxiety when they simply anticipate the situations they fear. This anticipatory anxiety escalates as a person approaches the frightening situation, thereby making it all the more stressful when it's finally confronted. This in turn increases the anticipatory anxiety the next time the circumstance is approached. In this way a cycle of escalating anxiety is established that over time can lead to complete isolation.

People with social phobia tend to be exquisitely sensitive to criticism or rejection, have low self-esteem, and difficulty asserting themselves. They often have trouble making eye contact, and, unfortunately, display easily observable signs of anxiety in social situations (cold, clammy hands, shaky voices and limbs). All this leads to difficulty in class participation and anxiety in test situations—and therefore to academic underachievement. Likewise, they lead to underachievement at work because of difficulty communicating or making presentations. Compared to their peers, their social lives are less developed and they are less likely to marry. In severe cases they drop out of school or work, have no friends, don't date, and remain with their family of origin.

Onset is usually in the mid-teens, though it can begin in early childhood. It may follow an especially stressful or humiliating experience, or its onset may be gradual. Its severity is usually continuous, though it may become less severe or remit altogether during adulthood. It may vary with increasing stresses or demands, becoming dormant during a good marriage, for example, and re-emerging with divorce or the death of a spouse. Job promotions, with their increased demands (especially for public speaking), may lead to a re-emergence of symptoms for someone who earlier had managed to avoid the activities that scare him. The condition is remarkably common, though this fact has been appreciated only in the last decade or so. Estimates of its prevalence run as high as thirteen percent of the population, making it the third most common psychiatric disorder (behind depression and alcoholism).

It's terribly important to know about social phobia. Since the condition responds to treatment, correctly identifying it in yourself or in others can lead to a remarkable change for the better.

Agoraphobia

This disorder (literally, a fear of open places) involves excessive anxiety about being in places or situations from which escape may be difficult or embarrassing. If the patient is prone to panic attacks (see below), he may fear being in places where help may not be available in the event of an attack (around ninety-five percent of patients with agoraphobia seen by psychiatrists have had panic attacks). Some people fear embarrassing symptoms like loss of bladder control or fainting. Since being alone makes the fearful situations much more frightening, the person often requires a partner. In people who suffer from panic attacks, the agoraphobia usually develops within a year or so of the first attack.

Agoraphobia can be devastating to career and personal life. In severe cases, a person can become completely housebound. The need for a special sort of partner can initiate or perpetuate a relationship based on the dependency of the person, the controllingness of the partner, or both.

Panic Attacks and Panic Disorder

A panic attack is a period of anxiety intense enough to cause complete immobilization. The attacks can occur with any of several disorders; if they recur repeatedly, the condition is called panic disorder. Estimates are that between 1.5 and 3 percent of the population will develop the disorder at some point in their lives. The attacks begin with the sudden onset of intense fear or unbearable discomfort, and build to a peak in ten minutes or less. They usually involve a sense of imminent catastrophe or of death, and a panicky urge to escape. They're usually accompanied by a number of physical symptoms of intense anxiety—including palpitations, sweating, trembling, shortness of breath, a sense of smothering or choking, chest pain, nausea, dizziness, feelings of unreality, chills or flushing, numbness and tingling, and a fear of losing control of one's mind. People often imagine they're dying from a heart attack or stroke.

Recurring panic attacks can completely shatter a person's emotional well-being. Many fear that they're suffering from an undiagnosed life-threatening illness, and remain frightened despite repeated medical testing and reassurance. They tend to avoid an increasing number of situations or places that remind them of the original panic—sometimes developing agoraphobia in the process. Some people become preoccupied with their health or with the loss of people they love. As their range of activities diminishes, demoralization typically follows. Many drop out of school or work. Some become dependent on illicit substances which they begin as attempts to treat the attacks. Over half of those with panic disorder eventually become depressed.

Generalized Anxiety Disorder (GAD)

A person with GAD worries and frets about anything and everything, and try as he might, he can't set the worries aside. At the same time, he's plagued by the physical signs of anxiety—restlessness; easy fatigability; irritability; muscle tension; sleep disturbance; cold, clammy hands; dry mouth; sweating; nausea; diarrhea; difficulty swallowing; a tendency to startle at the slightest surprise. Such people seem "as tight as a drum" or "wound up like a spring," images denoting the excessive tension and propensity to unwind into a tangled mass of complaint, worry, and doleful prophecy. Such people make those around them nervous, and this complicates interpersonal life. You might try to reason with them or calm them down, for example, only to find yourself countered and frustrated by an endless flow of "yes, but . . ." responses to well-intentioned advice or offers of assistance. Unfortunately, the person with GAD has no more control over his endless worry and pessimism than someone in the middle of a panic attack has over his terror. Knowing this can spare you a good deal of futility trying to reason with him about his state of mind. You need instead to get him to someone who can help him. Chapter Ten will outline some ways to do this.

The difference between GAD and panic disorder is one of intensity and duration. People unfortunate enough to suffer both GAD and panics (anxiety's counterpart to double depression), for example, sometimes describe life with GAD as one long panic attack. One way to understand these conditions, in fact, is to consider both GAD and panic attacks as conditions in which the body's normal emergency response to threat—the flight-or-fight response—has gotten out of control. In the normal operation of the flight-or-fight response, the brain prepares the body to respond to threat—the mind becomes alert and hypervigilant; the pupils dilate; respiratory and heart rates accelerate; blood is shunted to the heart, brain, and muscles; sphincters tighten (to escape without a trace); and so on. Those people whose flight-or-fight system fires too easily, then, are prone to panic attacks, and those whose systems can't shut down are prone to GAD. Fortunately there are a number of treatment approaches to help re-tune the system.

Obsessive-Compulsive Disorder (OCD)

Obsessions are thoughts, impulses, or images that may be meaningless or absurd but cannot be put out of one's mind. Compulsions are equally absurd or meaningless rituals that also cannot be resisted. OCD involves one or both of these. It typically begins in adolescence or later. Typical compulsive rituals include washing one's hands dozens of times a day, or checking repeatedly whether the gas is turned off when trying to leave the house. Obsessions are equally imperious; examples include a preoccupation with being contaminated by contact with harmless objects like doorknobs or coffee cups, impulses to kill or injure one's children, and other intrusive ideas or images. A person with OCD has no idea why these ideas or rituals are so imperative; he simply cannot resist them. Like the impulses to perform the rituals, the obsessive thoughts come unbidden. If the compulsive tries to resist his rituals, he feels a great deal of anxiety; eventually it becomes so intense that he has no choice but to submit.

Until the last decade or so, no one, certainly not psychiatrists, had any idea how common this disorder is—a circumstance that left many a person with OCD feeling that he was the only one to endure such a condition. The condition and its prevalence (around two percent of the population) are better understood today, but a great many people still suffer in silent ignorance about their condition.

The problem is complicated by popular confusion between two similar-sounding disorders: obsessive-compulsive disorder and the obsessive-compulsive personality. Obsessive-compulsive disorder is a psychiatric syndrome consisting of full-blown obsessions and compulsions. It has a well-established genetic and biological basis, and a number of effective treatments. Obsessive-compulsive personality is a kind of personality style with traits that approximate the obsessions and compulsions of OCD—but it does not involve full obsessions and compulsions. The person with obsessive-compulsive personality is preoccupied with order, frugality, and cleanliness; is stubborn, controlling, often stodgy and self-righteous; and sometimes completely humorless. Typically, his thinking is overly logical and minimally imaginative, framed in all black and white, with no shades of gray, no color. His fastidiousness, however, doesn't reach the point of compulsion. If he loses control of an enterprise, for example, he gets fussy and testy and is likely to storm off, but he's not incapacitated with anxiety as an OCD person would be if a compulsion is thwarted. On the other hand, people with OCD have a normal range of personality styles—well beyond that of the stodgy obsessive-compulsive personality. There's a greater percentage of OCD in antisocial personality, for example, than in obsessive-compulsive personalities.

For our purposes, the most important difference between obsessive-compulsive disorder and obsessive-compulsive personality is in their very different responses to treatment. An obsessive-compulsive personality responds to talking therapy, not to biological treatments. This treatment, however, takes a long time to soften the stony rigidity, controllingness, and tightfistedness of the typical obsessive-compulsive personality. It's not unusual for the psychoanalysis of an obsessive-compulsive character to take a decade or more, five times a week—and even then the changes aren't always very palpable, at least not from the outside. OCD, on the other hand, can often be controlled in a matter of weeks (or less) with medication or behavioral treatment. If you're in a relationship with an obsessive-compulsive personality, you're likely to face a lifetime of control struggles and immaculate tidiness, rock-solid stubbornness and near-superhuman stability, dour sobriety and unshakable commitment—a set of trade-offs that, all things considered, you may prefer. Just go in with your eyes open. If, on the other hand, you're in, or are considering, a relationship with a person with OCD, how the relationship goes will depend largely on whether his OCD is treated.

Posttraumatic Stress Disorder (PTSD)

PTSD is a syndrome that follows exposure to an extremely traumatic situation—like someone's death, the threat of one's own death, or serious injury. The response involves extreme fear and feelings of helplessness and horror. Over time it includes persistent re-experiencing of the traumatic event (in recurrent illusions, intrusive memories, nightmares, and flashback experiences). It also comes to involve avoidance of situations resembling or symbolizing the trauma, a general numbing of responsiveness, and persistent symptoms of arousal (difficulty sleeping, irritability, hypervigilance, exaggerated startle response). By definition, the syndrome persists for more than a month—but it usually goes on much longer.

Events leading to PTSD include military combat, rape, violent assault, kidnapping, being taken hostage, terrorist attacks, torture, severe automobile accidents, and in children, inappropriate and coercive sexual experiences. The ongoing re-experiencing of the trauma, emotional numbing, and avoidance of associations to the trauma interfere with relationships and often lead to marital conflict and divorce, along with work problems and job loss.

Dealing with Anxiety Disorders in Yourself and Others

It's important to understand that I'm writing about anxiety disorders, not about the ordinary anxiety that's a part of everyone's life every day. To learn to deal with it in yourself and others is a big part of growing up, and growing up takes a lifetime—and I doubt there's much I can add here to hurry the process along. A few general remarks may help, though, as well as set in context what I can say about dealing with anxiety disorders.

On the one hand, you have to understand that anxiety is there to help—like the time it warned me about the rattlesnake. Thus, if you find yourself getting anxious, look around, so to speak, and try to learn why. Have you forgotten to pick up your wife after work? Are you procrastinating too long about that assignment they dumped on you? On the other hand, if you find yourself being pushed around by a specific anxiety that you know is excessive, you'll need to deal with it the same way you deal with any other bully—stand up to it. If you're anxious (but not phobic) about, say, speaking in front of a church group, or entering a dance contest, do it anyway. If you hold back because you're afraid you won't do so well, then you'll never learn that you can do the thing you were so anxious about—and, more important, that even if you don't do it perfectly, things will turn out just fine anyway.

If your anxiety is more serious than the minor ones I've just mentioned, psychotherapy may help you. Finding yourself too anxious about going back to school to let yourself apply, or too nervous around people you're attracted to to get to know them—these anxieties probably relate to your upbringing and how it's affected you, and can be unraveled over time by working with a good therapist. The fact that severe disorders like OCD or panic attacks can be treated so much more easily than milder problems like obsessive-compulsive personality or ordinary nervousness seems paradoxical (and unfair)—but it's true anyway.

Identifying an anxiety disorder isn't as difficult as identifying a mood disorder, or even ADD. The symptoms are absolutely straightforward. By definition, if you're phobic or have obsessions or compulsions, you know that your symptoms are irrational. If you have panic attacks, or symptoms of PTSD, you can't miss them, or the diagnosis.

One aspect of identifying the anxiety disorders, however, must be emphasized. Each of the disorders we've considered so far can be simulated by a number of medical conditions. Most serious cardiac or pulmonary disorders generate a good deal of anxiety, and can look for all the world like GAD or panic disorder. I raise the issue here because the medical conditions that simulate anxiety disorders are among the most serious. Many can be life threatening in very short order, like a myocardial infarction or angina, pulmonary emboli, malignant hypertension, intracranial hemorrhages, among others. Thus, if you feel anxious and have a serious physical symptom like chest pain, shortness of breath, or a loss of consciousness, don't assume you have an anxiety disorder (however much that idea may comfort you)—get medical help fast. If it proves to be a false alarm, great.

Having eliminated medical causes, your next step is to allow yourself to get help. Easier said than done. Many people feel they should be able to get a grip on themselves, pull themselves up by the bootstraps, and solve the problems themselves. But having an anxiety disorder is not a character weakness; it's a specific disorder of a specific set of chemicals in specific locations and connections in your brain. It isn't your fault and it isn't your responsibility to solve it without the right tools. You deserve appropriate help for a panic attack in the same way that you would get help for, say, the adrenal tumor or thyroid storm that can simulate one.

There are several effective treatments for the anxiety disorders—medication, behavioral techniques, and a number of newer techniques. Older techniques, like psychoanalysis and other talking therapies, aren't as useful. Chapter Eleven will elaborate the options.

The next several chapters survey the many ways the disorders we've discussed can distort and disrupt relationships, as well as put them out of reach altogether.

CHAPTER 5

How Your Brain Can Get You into the Wrong Relationship

The story of Wendell and Marion Satterly in Chapter Two showed how ADD can pull people together for the wrong reasons. Wendell, on the one hand, needed organizing and caretaking from the maternal, controlling Marion. His ADD so disrupted his thought process, however, that he didn't think through what sort of relationship was likely to follow in the wake of his neediness. Marion, on the other hand, was drawn to Wendell's brilliant potential, and imagined that with but a touch of her organizational talent, it would propel him to the great things she needed so badly to share. She didn't understand, however, how costly this subsidiary role would be to her own development, or how difficult a man like Wendell could be to live with. Unfortunately, relationships like this are common when one or both partners has any of the psychiatric disorders we've discussed so far. The disorders generate a special sort of neediness—and therefore a special sort of seductiveness to the other person who, for his own reasons, feels drawn to fill the needs involved.

This chapter looks at these relationships from both sides: from that of the person with the disorder and from that of the person who may get involved with him. Chapters Two through Four suggested ways to identify psychiatric disorders in oneself or one's partner. Here we'll explore how someone who knows he has one of the disorders can avoid getting himself into a bad relationship, or how another person can avoid being drawn into a bad relationship with him. We'll ask, too, what it is about each condition that can pull you into a relationship that's doomed to fail. Finally, we'll explore what you can do if you're already in a relationship and have come to realize that a psychiatric condition you weren't even aware of pulled you into it—and for all the wrong reasons.

We'll search out the answers by looking at a pair of typical examples. In each case we'll look at both what went wrong and what went right. In addition, we'll address questions that worry most people who come for help: suppose treatment changes me, will my partner still want me? Will I still want him? Or (worries the partner) suppose she gets treated—will she still need me? Fortunately, the cases show that the answers depend mostly on what the two of you do. It's also fortunate that with treatment most of them turn out like the Balusteris of Chapter One: With enough effort, both partners can adjust so that the relationship can reshape itself into a much better one. We'll look carefully at what you can do to increase your chances of moving toward a good relationship—or of getting out of a hopelessly bad one in time.

What Gets You into the Mess: The Larsons

Mary O'Toole's ill-advised decision to marry David Larson illuminates many of the themes of this chapter. Mary, a thirty-five-year-old engineer, was sent for consultation by her marriage counselor because she thought Mary was depressed and that antidepressant medication might help her. The couple had been married for five years, and from all appearances, were doing well. Mary said they were both happy in the marriage, and that she was in treatment to work out whether to have children, not because there were interpersonal problems. She wasn't able to discuss the emotional aspects of her marriage very well, but no less well than any other Silicon Valley engineer—male or female.

When Mary first came in, it seemed clear that she was quite

depressed. Her tearfulness, hopelessness, fatigue, and difficulty with sleep and concentration led me to suggest a course of antidepressant medication—and she agreed. After a few weeks she felt much better: more alert, energetic, better able to concentrate. I saw her every month or so for short follow-up appointments. During our sixth session Mary announced that she'd found a new diagnosis for herself. She'd read an article about ADD and felt she fit the syndrome perfectly. I agreed completely. I had asked about problems with attention when she'd first come in, but her depression had seemed to account for whatever problem she had with it. Typical of ADD patients, her poor memory had kept her from remembering the trouble that ADD had caused all her life, and the ADD was mild enough so that she could focus her attention during our meetings by sheer force of will.

Medication for ADD and depression can be taken simultaneously. Therefore we added a course of medication for ADD, and her response was very gratifying—except that after three days her two-week supply of pills was used up. She called, embarrassed, and said that she must have misplaced them or else someone must have taken them from her desk at work. ADD patients routinely lose or misplace their medication (along with everything else), so I wasn't too concerned. She hid the second bottle of medication at home, but again over half the supply disappeared within a few days. The only one who could have taken them, she said, was her husband, David. She asked him about it, but he denied knowing anything about the pills.

Mary told me all this with a great deal of anxiety. Was it possible that he could do such a thing? As she thought about this, it surprised her how clear her thinking had become since starting treatment for her ADD. David, she could now understand, had undoubtedly done things like this repeatedly over the last five years: stealing from her and others, routinely staying out late, disappearing for days and spending large amounts of money with flimsy explanations, and so on. She now understood that each time she confronted him, he would deny any misdeed and then report (or provoke) some crisis that would distract her from the matter at hand. Each time she'd forget about the original incident. This time, as she asked him about the missing pills, a phone call interrupted their conversation. David said that it was his brother with terrible news: He'd been tested HIV positive. Instead of her usual response of getting upset and disorganized, and then dropping the matter at hand, Mary calmly pushed the call-back sequence on the phone (this feature returns the call to the caller without revealing his number). She noted that only seven digits beeped (the brother had a different area code—so there should have been ten beeps), and that a woman answered. Mary asked for David. An awkward pause preceded a brusque reply that she had the wrong number. She didn't confront David at the time but instead came to my office to discuss the matter.

Now the tables had turned. David, with his lying, stealing, and infidelity, was now the patient. Mary was the mentally healthy partner, and had to decide what to do about him. She tried to understand what was wrong with David, and felt that making an appointment for both of them would be the best way to hear his side of the story.

David did indeed tell his story—and it was sobering. Yes, he'd taken the Ritalin and yes, he'd sold it—mostly to high school kids who in turn sold it to younger kids. So? And yes, he'd been unfaithful—dozens of times. Who hadn't? He said that he'd chosen Mary because she'd been so intoxicated with his good looks and smooth manner that she was an easy mark. It was clear that he'd been coolly calculating in his choice of Mary for a wife. He knew that she had a very low opinion of herself, and that she felt fortunate to have someone like him. He knew a more secure woman would look beneath his smoothly polished surface and reject him for what she found. He also knew that Mary was hopelessly disorganized in her professional and personal life, and that he could therefore become indispensable to her by helping her establish some order in her life—and that this would take only a minimal effort for someone like him. He said all this with a cool indifference, feeling no guilt whatever for having taken such unconscionable advantage of his wife's weaknesses. Listening to him, Mary was by turns astonished, enraged, and vindictive, and over the course of a few days decided to leave him.

I chose the story of Mary and David because it highlights three general effects of psychiatric disorders that pull people into relationships that are unlikely to do well. First is the low self-esteem that results from any psychiatric disorder. Anyone who doesn't feel good about himself is at a terrible disadvantage entering a relationship. He feels that he doesn't have much to offer and therefore doesn't deserve a desirable partner. He also feels that he doesn't deserve to be treated well, and he therefore can't protect himself from exploitative tendencies in a potential partner. Mary was especially vulnerable in this regard. She felt unattractive, uninteresting, and unintelligent—none of which was true. Feeling this way about herself, she felt fortunate to have won such an attractive man as David. As David had known, a woman with a more secure sense of herself would have looked at him more carefully and seen how unattractive he was in the areas that really matter in a long-term relationship—integrity, reliability, the capacity for love and reciprocity, and so on.

A second effect of any psychiatric disorder is an exaggerated need for caretaking: A person with ADD, for example, can't organize himself or his affairs, a depressed person can't comfort or care for himself, an anxious person can't face the world alone. Thus a person with a psychiatric disorder needs a good deal of care but doesn't feel good enough about himself to feel that he deserves it. His partner will usually have mixed feelings of her own about taking care of someone like this. Thus, the relationship becomes a mutually conflicted sort of child-parent relationship, with each partner having mixed feelings about the degree of caretaking involved, and ultimately about each other. Because of her ADD and depression, Mary felt especially needy of someone to organize and comfort her. What she found, however, was someone whose intention was to control and exploit her.

A third effect of all significant psychiatric disorders results from the intrinsic limitations of whatever disorder a person has. Like Wendell Satterly, a person with ADD can be too scattered to understand what a partner is like or what's likely to be good or bad in the relationship with her. If anything, he's likely to idealize the partner as a savior. Like a person with ADD, an overly anxious person can also be too scattered and distracted by his need for comforting to understand his partner. Mary's depression and ADD set her up to connect with someone like David. The ADD kept her from thinking carefully enough about David to understand his serious limitations, and the low self-esteem from her depression made her feel that she didn't deserve someone who had more to offer than David.

Fortunately, relationships that begin for all the wrong reasons sometimes turn out fine in the long run—but it takes some work. To explore what partners can do to bring about a good outcome despite an ill-advised beginning, I'll present a couple who did what it took to make their relationship work. In the final section I'll use what we've learned from the two couples to generate a list of guidelines for getting yourself through this kind of ordeal.

How to Get out of the Mess: The Gardners

Unlike Mary, Joan Gardner found out surprisingly early in her marriage that she'd made a serious mistake choosing Lance— on her wedding night. After a few rounds of sexual festivity in the cabin they'd rented for the week, she told Lance that she was very happy but very worn out—and fell asleep. A few hours later she awoke to find him gone. Frightened—the cabin was one of three or four in an isolated area up the California coast—she peered out into the moonlit night, and nearly fainted dead away. Lance was standing, on tiptoe, next to the window of another cabin—naked and masturbating. When she chased him down and dragged him back, he calmly explained that he liked to masturbate watching couples have sex just as much as he liked having sex with couples—which he liked much more than having it with individuals. Really? Didn't he think this was a bit out of line? No, he didn't. Did he do it often? Yes, he did. Why hadn't he told her this? It never came up. What else did he do like this? Oh, a lot of things . . .

He went on to describe a Britannica's worth of sexual exploits, menages, voyeurism, and other unusual (for Joan, anyway) activity. He felt no embarrassment or regret whatsoever, and couldn't understand Joan's consternation. After a time he fell off to sleep, leaving her to pace and cry, fret and ponder throughout the rest of the night about just what she'd gotten herself into. During their courtship, she had been so swept up in Lance's spontaneity and boyish enthusiasm that it didn't occur to her that it might be accompanied by anything as grandly pornographic as he'd just described. She'd been engaged once to a man much like herself, but the engagement ended as much from the sheer tedium of two people so hopelessly inhibited as from anything else. Lance was just the opposite, and therefore seemed perfect for her. She just hadn't thought it through.

But still! What was the matter with *him?*

That question completely stumped her—and she spent the rest of the night and of the honeymoon week agonizing about it. When they got home, she called her family doctor for advice, and was sent to me. She brought Lance with her. In the first hour they elaborated the events of their wedding night and something of their personal histories. I did my best to explain that, yes, Joan was a very inhibited person, but that she was right about Lance— there was indeed something wrong with him. His behavior and history left no doubt that whatever else might be troublesome about his personality, Lance was very attention disordered. I told them in colloquial terms, and as gently as I could, that he had a severe case of ADD, along with an unusually intense set of psychological responses to it. These included a frantic need for sexual activity to dispel the boredom and restlessness resulting from his ADD. Over time his sexual impulses had developed a life of their own—as such powerful impulses always do—in this case in the direction of sexual exploration and conquest, along with a driven voyeurism and other mildly perverse expressions of his sexual urges. Joan, on the other hand, seemed relatively healthy emotionally—except for a certain degree of sexual naïveté and inhibition, mostly culturally determined—that (I admit) was refreshing after hearing about Lance's set of more sophisticated escapades. They listened to what I said, and decided that they would like to go into treatment.

Treating Lance for ADD worked well. He now channeled his prodigious sexual energy into making love only with Joan. Consequently she no longer felt in competition with the entire universe of sexual activity. At the same time, treatment increased Lance's capacity to concentrate on his work, let him read much more easily, elevated his self-esteem, and in general made his life much more organized.

His reaction to all this was mixed though—he was pleased with how well he could concentrate and with how good Joan felt about it all, but he nonetheless missed the excitement of his old sex life. He felt as if he was losing all his old friends (his symptoms, that is to say). On the other hand, he knew he was getting a new best friend—and he said he preferred Joan to the old friends (I suspect it was by a closer margin than he let on—but I let it go). Joan also had mixed feelings. She was happy that Lance set aside the wild life, but it worried her that even with medication he still didn't feel that anything was wrong with what he'd been doing. He'd given it up, that is to say as a matter of practical necessity not of principle. On the whole though, Joan felt that there was enough she loved about Lance that it didn't make sense to leave him for one character flaw (however monumental). As long as he promised to take his medication and to be faithful to her, it seemed right to her. And over the year or so since I met them, they have stayed married and remain happy about their choice.

What to Do/How to Be

Why did Mary and David's relationship unravel whereas Lance and Joan's persisted intact? In a way, Mary never had a chance for a good relationship (I'm identifying Mary and Lance as our patients here). Mary's ADD and depression affected her in such a way that she couldn't assess a potential partner adequately. She was so poor at assessing men, in fact, that if she'd made a good choice for a partner, her success would have been based largely on good fortune. Lance's ADD, on the other hand, didn't seem to affect his ability to select an appropriate partner, and for all the right reasons (see below). Put another way, Mary's brain let her down. Thus a major lesson is that disorders like ADD and depression greatly diminish a person's capacity to make a good choice of a partner—and ideally should be treated before a person chooses a partner.

Unfortunately, there's nothing we can do about what disorders we inherit or what sort of luck we have. We can, however, prepare ourselves to avoid bad choices by learning as much as we can about the psychological factors that helped Lance and Joan save their relationship and let David and Mary's fail. A good place to start is with a difference between Mary and Lance that is so important it will form the basis of a major theme running through much of this book. It can be understood in terms of the general effects of psychiatric disorders I listed earlier: a lowered self-esteem, an exaggerated need for caretaking, and limitations imposed by the disorder itself. Mary, on the one hand—however mild her symptoms seemed to be—needed a partner to help her overcome them. She chose David, hoping (foolishly, and only half consciously) that his graceful sociability and personal attractiveness would make her feel better about herself, that he would take care of her, and that he would help her get organized. Lance, on the other hand—no matter how egregious his symptoms seemed to be—dealt with the same problems almost entirely within his own psychology. That is, as paradoxical as it may sound at first blush, his solutions (promiscuity, voyeurism) didn't require his partner to be a prop for his self-esteem, need for caretaking, and limitations from ADD. Therefore, he was able to form a largely healthy relationship with Joan that was independent of his psychological needs and symptoms. This was in sharp contrast to Mary, whose psychological problems (and choice of a partner based on them) did not allow a healthy relationship, independent of her needs, to develop between her and David.

As I said, at first glance this idea may seem paradoxical, since Lance was so much more theatrically disturbed than Mary—but it's true nonetheless. In fact, the degree to which a partner can contain his difficulties within his own personality (or even within his own symptoms) and therefore spare his partner an entanglement with them can be a good predictor of how well a relationship will do. Unfortunately (and I'm sure the reader will agree), it's a concept that's not so easy to apply (though as we go along the idea will seem more intuitive). Fortunately, it's much easier to see the beneficial effects of what the containment of needs and symptoms does for a relationship. These are the things that Lance and Joan had going for them that Mary and David didn't. I'll list them:

They liked each other, and liked being with each other.

This is so basic that it's easy to overlook. Joan did get a thrill out of Lance's flamboyance and disinhibition, but her main reason for wanting to marry him was that she liked him and liked being with him. Lance was turned on by Joan's sexy good looks, but he (of all people) knew that there are lots of sexy women—he wanted to marry Joan because he liked being with her. Thus when something went wrong, they were fond enough of each other and had enough in common that Joan could accept Lance's problems and Lance could give up his wild outside life to stay with her. This wasn't the case with Mary and David. Mary was drawn to David's sexy unconventionality, and to his ability to take care of her. David was drawn to Mary physically, but even more to her talent as a chump. But neither liked or respected much about the other. Whereas Lance found spending time with Joan made up for the loss of his outside activities, it seems unlikely that David would feel that spending time with Mary made up for the lost thrills of abusing stimulants and having affairs.

They accepted the problem for what it was, and were willing to do what they needed to solve it.

Accepting the problem involved something different for each partner. For Lance, it meant respecting Joan's opinion that there was a problem and that something was wrong with him. For Joan, it involved accepting that something was very wrong with Lance but being willing to learn about it—and not automatically rejecting him because he's flawed. Mary took the step of accepting that something was wrong with David and, if David were the sort of person who would (or could) do what he could to develop emotionally, the relationship might have had a chance. But he isn't.

They accepted treatment.

It's one thing to acknowledge something's wrong with you and another to get it treated. Many people drop the ball at this point, citing a variety of reasons or rationalizations. Behind all these there usually lurks a lingering reluctance to believe that there's a problem—as long as someone doesn't act on the idea, deep down he can still deny to himself that anything is wrong.

They were willing to set aside the pleasures of their pathology.

The most important element in saving the Gardners' marriage was Lance's willingness to put aside the adolescent thrills of his sexual misadventures. If he were to give his marriage a chance, David would have had to do the same with the thrills of using speed and the other misconduct that goes with it. He wasn't.

At first this doesn't sound applicable to disorders (like ADD or dysthymia) that don't involve drug highs, sexual excesses, or other thrills. But absurd as it sounds, people do become attached to their symptoms just as if they were old friends and don't like to give them up. Some symptoms, of course, no one would miss: We can all do without panic attacks, for example, or compulsions telling us to kill our children. These, however, are the exceptions. As we saw in Chapter Two, for example, many depressed people feel that their suffering makes them superior—like Job, they imagine that their suffering makes them special and will win them admiration and sympathy. Or they up the ante and annoy others with their gloom and lamentations to the point that their victims either leave or lash out in self-defense. Then they feel morally superior for putting up with such abuse. As we've seen throughout, people (especially depressed people) prefer feeling good about themselves to simply feeling good—and will therefore hold on to whatever symptoms they can misuse for that purpose.

Naturally enough, then, the fourth item we've listed is a common sticking place in a couple's attempts to get a derailed relationship back on track.

"Children" and Their Baby-Sitters: What to Do

Though each psychiatric disorder affects people differently, there's a common denominator: The patient becomes more like a child. It's worth understanding this process in some detail—whether you're the partner with the disorder or the one who has to deal with someone who has it. The inconsolable despair of a depressive, for example, is much like that of a two- or three-year-old whose mother has left, even if for a moment. As I'm writing this, for example, my two-year-old daughter, Rachel, is huddled in my lap, head buried in my chest, crying miserably for her mommy. Mommy's just gone out for the mail, but Rachel looks and sounds as if she's gone forever. I can't console her (daddies are useless at such times), though she's starting to get a little distracted by the scribblings on the paper. A depression brings the terrible (and terribly vulnerable) two-year-old back in ascendance as it eclipses the more sensible set of adult emotional responses.

It's the same with OCD: The pointless preoccupations or absurd rituals become much less mysterious after you've tried to reason with a two-year-old. A few months ago, Rachel's twin, Daniel, was obsessed with tennis racquets. He carried three of them around everywhere: eating breakfast, chasing his brother, climbing trees, taking baths—and least negotiably, sleeping at night. More recently he spotted a little parrot ladder in a pet store (a four-inch three-runged item for the bird to climb on), and he had to have it. *Had* to. He threw a tantrum of such thermonuclear proportions that (to save the species) I gave in and bought it for him. He played with nothing else for two days and two nights. Then he decided he needed a "big, big, huge one ladu," and spoke of nothing else for two more days until he got his way again (this time with a twenty-four-rung four-foot "ladu" which he dragged, climbed, clobbered, and slept with the next several weeks). The mad imperiousness and absolute irrationality of the obsessive-compulsive patient who has to line up the salad forks end to end or sleep next to seven bookshelves, then, doesn't seem so strange to someone who's matched wills with the likes of Daniel—and in fact that's precisely what a fork-stacking OCD patient is when under the spell of his compulsions: a grown adult, much of whose personality is out of commission except for its role in carrying around a two-year-old Daniel whose whims run the show.

It's the same for the other disorders. The phobic patient relives the irrational fears of the young child, the ADD patient has the attention span of a young child, and so on. Freud called this effect regression. The trouble is that while Daniel and Rachel will grow out of their infantile behavior, the adult won't—as long as he's affected by his psychiatric disorder. A relationship with a seriously depressed person, for example, involves giving endless comfort and consolation to an adult who cries like a baby but has none of a baby's charm. The disorder has brought out a person's childlike aspects so completely that little of an adult emotional life remains. All the patient wants from a partner, then, is a baby-sitter. I state the matter in these terms because the unflattering images of Child and baby-sitter will help fix the ideas in mind, and because they're accurate as guides for determining if you're in one of the roles (I capitalize Child to avoid confusion with the real item).

This idea is especially important if you find that your current predicament is but one in a long line of similar predicaments—in which you're playing the Child or the baby-sitter over and over. The prototypic babysitter, for example, is the daughter of an alcoholic father whose adult love life is a string of relationships with half a dozen alcoholics whom she's tried, and failed, to rehabilitate. The sooner she learns that each new man is the latest incarnation of her father, the better. She also needs to learn as soon as possible that deeper down she's seeking each time the martyrish self-satisfaction that her mother found in many years of beatings, infidelities, and abandonments by her drunken husband.

On the other side of the coin is the prototypic Child: the chronic depressive whose neediness and lack of reciprocity loses him girlfriend after girlfriend. He needs to learn that it's the self-centered, hungry little two-year-old in him that drains the energy, enthusiasm, and eventually the love out of anyone close to him. It's too much to expect that such a person will understand on his own how unbalanced a relationship he demands—even though each girlfriend tells him that repeatedly. If, however, he does learn (from friends, books, therapists) that the basis of his miserable relationships is a set of symptoms of his chronic depression, then he has a chance to have the depression treated and his relationships put back in balance. As treatment for his depression restores the more adult aspects of his personality, he'll become a much less needy and less self-centered partner.

Thus we'll need to look carefully at what to do from both sides of Child/baby-sitter relationships like those of the Larsons or the Gardners.

If You're the Baby-Sitter

The first thing to do, of course, is to figure out if it's a Child you're dealing with. Are you giving, giving, giving and getting nothing in return? Is your new partner interested only in being years. What makes it vicarious, then, is the identification without the participation. To be fair to Howard, vicarious thrills are normal enough in sports fans (if not overdone), and help make it fun to follow sports. But not in a love relationship. To whatever extent you play Howard to your partner's Joe, your relationship is the worse for it. Even if Joan were content to stand on the sidelines and marvel (or cheerlead) at Lance's foward passes, so to speak, sooner or later she'd feel left out and come to resent it.

To her credit, what she did instead was get off the sidelines. She took a hard look at herself and realized that if she were to live with Lance (with or without medication), she would have to get past her own sexual inhibitions. She resolved to get treatment with a specialist in this area. Over a relatively short time she became much less inhibited—and consequently less in awe of Lance's complete lack of inhibition.

If you suspect the answer to this last question is yes, then you need to decide whether you share your partner's exuberance, impishness or other childlike traits as a participant who can play along, or from the sidelines as someone who can't. Do you, for example, watch him show off, be flirtatious, or enjoy himself without guilt and wish you could be that way but can't? If it's yes, then be careful—because eventually you're going to resent him, and the resentment will erode the relationship more and more over time. Your job is to see what's keeping the childlike parts of your personality on the sidelines—any good relationship needs a good deal of play between the child in you and in your partner. If thinking about it or discussing it with friends (including your partner) doesn't free up the problem, it may be time to consult a professional.

Do you feel, deep down, that your suffering and persistence as a baby-sitter make you superior?

This issue is more subtle, but ultimately more problematic than the preceding one—partly because people rarely recognize their devotion to pride and vanity, and partly because, even if they do recognize it, they are extremely hard to give up. Nonetheless, it's worth a try—with or without counseling (it's easier with).

The danger sign is the self-serving sense of superiority, of saintliness, in your long suffering with your problem-child partner. One giveaway is catching yourself thinking how much people must admire your selflessness and perseverance. "What a strong woman she is," a patient of mine imagined her neighbors were thinking as they watched and disapproved of her husband's drunken, promiscuous behavior. She didn't know that I was treating one of her neighbors—whose only thoughts on the matter were that she was a fool and that her husband was great in bed.

In keeping with her upbringing, Joan was indeed tempted by feelings of moral superiority toward Lance. She was honest enough with herself, though, to admit that she wasn't superior—she was simply more repressed. She didn't, therefore, resist Lance's improvement with treatment in order to maintain a sense of superiority.

If You're the Child

It isn't fair to put Child and baby-sitter on the same plane here. Real infants can't understand their deficiencies, and neither can most people with significant psychiatric disorders. If a depressed person is told he's being too self-centered in his endless complaints or too pessimistic in his visions of gloom, he simply thinks you don't understand him and his situation. Still, the more perspective you can get on your own contribution to your troubles, the better. Thus, if you find yourself wondering if you've been playing the Child role, or, if you've been told this by a partner (or, especially, a series of partners), you'd better ask yourself three questions corresponding to the ones we asked the baby-sitters.

Is the baby-sitter/Child interaction the basis of your relationship?

You've first got to ask yourself if one trait seems to be undoing all your relationships. If you've been dumped a dozen times by people who tell you that you're too needy, for example, you'd better consider that it might be a symptom of depression—and get it evaluated and treated (if it is depression). If you've been told by a dozen people over the years that they hate the way you flake out on them and unravel whatever order they've put into your relationship, you'd better wonder if you have ADD—and then go for consultation. If the people you date run for cover when they learn that you can't go to work until you alphabetize the items in your refrigerator, you'd better ask someone who knows about OCD if you have it (very likely), and if you can get treated for it (absolutely).

If one of these seems to fit, and if it seems (or if you've been told) that there wasn't much you gave back for putting your partner through one of these ordeals, then you've been playing the Child. One of the psychiatric disorders has put the Child in you in charge, and treatment can get the adult back in control.

If you (or your partner or your doctor) feel that you aren't complying with treatment, you'll need to wonder if there are hidden gratifications in your symptoms—and that you don't want to give them up. Specifically:

Do you enjoy the vicarious effect your partner gets out of your symptoms?

Like Lance, some people get a thrill out of shocking their partners. They're like the little boy who amuses his parents by running naked through Macy's or by telling his teacher to "chill out" if she tries to discipline him. If his parents, for their own emotional reasons, got a charge out of this sort of thing, and their child knew it, he may try to shock or titillate people well past childhood. In doing this, he assumes (subconsciously) that his partner, like his parents, will delight in his naughtiness. In Joan's case, this wasn't true; she was horrified by Lance's wild behavior. It's much to Lance's credit that he learned this from her, took it to heart, and learned to get himself under better control.

Do your symptoms make you feel superior?

We all make virtues out of necessities. People like Lance, for example, feel that they're superior because they lack healthy inhibitions. They don't understand that what they call freedom is really a pathological inability to control themselves. At the opposite end of the scale, an obsessional feels superior because of his ironclad self-control. A chronically depressed spinster may pride herself on rejecting all the pleasures that deep down she'd love to have.

Lance avoided this trap. His admitting that his sexual cornucopia was a problem, not a virtue, gave his marriage a chance to work. David was not able to take this step.

In the next chapter we turn to relationships that unlike the ones in this chapter, started well but got torpedoed and sunk by the emergence of a psychiatric disorder.

CHAPTER 6

How Your Brain Can Ruin a Good Relationship

Most relationships start out well enough, but in most cases sooner or later something goes wrong, and they fall apart. Though a variety of misfortunes can do this, this chapter deals with only one—the onset of a psychiatric disorder in one of the partners. Unfortunately, this is a very common cause of relationships failing. The most common troublemakers are manic or depressive episodes, though the same thing can happen with the onset of OCD, any of the phobias, panic attacks, or a previously dormant post-traumatic stress reaction. The onset of PMS each month is an example of the process on a short-term repetitive basis, and may be the most common example of all. Even though ADD is a chronic condition, an increase in its severity can simulate the onset of a new disorder. Any increase in the complexity or chaos of one's life can bring this about—the birth of a child, for example, or a promotion (or demotion) at work are common examples.

Sometimes there's no apparent cause for the onset of the disorder, though a stressful event usually marks the onset of symptoms. A loss, for example, is the most common precipitant of a manic or depressive episode. A traumatic event can bring on a phobic disorder and, of course, PTSD—though there may be a period of delay between the event and the post-traumatic response.

How well a relationship survives the emergence of one of these disorders depends on the resilience of the partners and of the relationship. This chapter suggests what partners can do to preserve their relationship in this situation. I'll organize the discussion around two cases. In the first, the partners adjust in a way that preserves the relationship in the face of a number of psychiatric problems. In the second, the partners do not adjust well enough, and their problems undo the relationship. The contrast between how the two couples addressed their problems will help show how helpful the influence of common sense, mutual respect, education, and maturity are in these circumstances. Based on the examples, I'll suggest what to do if a psychiatric disorder ambushes your relationship.

In our first case, depression appears in both partners.

Jack and Sonia—the Marriage of Art and Science

Jack O'Shawnasee was a young poet and, like most young poets, was flat broke all the time. Unlike the more pedagogical Wendell Satterly, Jack couldn't support himself by teaching—he was much too shy and self-conscious to speak in front of a class. Thus, after graduating from an Ivy League College, he moved to California to write in solitude. He supported himself with a number of part-time jobs, like delivering flowers or making pizzas, that freed his mind to dream and create, unperturbed by the din of practicality—or, in less poetic terms, by other people. He moved into a cabin overlooking a sleepy vineyard in the hills behind Santa Cruz, and did odd jobs on the grounds in lieu of rent. His poverty Jack dismissed as romantic, and his self-imposed loneliness and isolation as part of his Gaelic temperament and heritage. However rationalized, the lifestyle fit perfectly, and allowed his work to flourish. His daydreams throughout the workday bore poetic fruit in the night when he would write and revise, revise and rewrite his poems and plays to his satisfaction. After about a year, he felt ready to publish his poems, and felt that he was about to make a name for himself in the literary world.

As later developments proved, Jack was indeed a fine writer, but his romanticized justifications for his secluded lifestyle were a sham. He lived alone because he was terribly sensitive to other people, a trait that had made his years at the bustling East Coast university a nightmare. The gentlest rejection, disapproval, or even challenge to his ideas or writing would sink him into an hour- or day-long funk that undid him and his capacity to work completely. Because of this sensitivity, Jack, now approaching thirty, had never had an enduring relationship, and had had only a few close friends. He was susceptible to excessively hurt feelings and depression in response to rejection. This combination of persistent shyness and depressive response to rejection have been found to respond well to a number of medications, and poorly to talking therapy. But Jack was much more interested in romanticizing his problems than in treating them, and so his life remained extremely lonely—if productive poetically.

Until he met Sonia. At first blush (quite literally, since Sonia too was very shy) she was as different from Jack as one could imagine. Recently from Kiev, Ukraine, Sonia Vinogradov was a graduate student in astrophysics, about a year away from finishing her doctorate, when she met Jack. Completely unlike him, she was practicality incarnate—a virtuoso with the complex technology of her field and with its very complex mathematical foundations. But like Jack her social life was a vacuum, though her rationalization for this was different from his—she thought that socializing, recreation, even enjoying the liberal arts were needless distractions from her beloved scientific studies. Beneath this veneer, however, was the barely subliminal awareness that she was vulnerable to spells of depression that frightened her—and that social life, with its inevitable disappointments and disillusionments, had the potential to bring on one of these depressions. These had begun in late adolescence and, since she'd avoided social situations so completely, were precipitated only by academic setbacks. Sonia's impossibly strict standards made disappointments in her work very frequent despite its consistently outstanding quality in all eyes but hers. It never occurred to Sonia, either in Kiev or in California, to seek help for her depressions. Rather, she got herself out of them by immersing herself in hard work. Unfortunately, this left her with a need to excel at ever more difficult academic challenges. Though she was not aware of it, her life was devoted almost completely to fending off the spectre of depression lurking just off the edge of her awareness. Until she met Jack.

Jack swept Sonia off her feet literally (with his bicycle), picked her up, and, as young people say in these circumstances, one thing led to another and they were married within the year.

Nothing stabilizes a mood disorder like a good relationship, and nothing stabilizes a good relationship like each partner's doing well outside the relationship. Thus, the first two years of Jack and Sonia's marriage were idyllic. Their differences in temperament and interests enriched their relationship as each came to respect, and to some degree master, much of the other's areas of expertise. By the end of the first two years of marriage, Sonia had completed her doctorate and taken a post-doctoral fellowship at her laboratory. Jack had published two books of poetry and was about to produce his first play at a major theater.

Nonetheless, lurking beneath all the success and good feelings were the emotional vulnerabilities that had plagued both Jack and Sonia during less happy times. Sonia's ongoing enchantment with Jack had protected his sensitivity to withdrawal or rejection, and her ongoing success in her work kept her own sensitivity to lapses in productivity well out of sight. Beyond this, the exceptional quality of Jack's work shielded him from the sort of negative reviews young writers often endure, thereby keeping his sensitivity to criticism from surfacing. Nothing goes smoothly forever, though, especially with so much sensitivity just beneath the surface. It was only a matter of time before some bump in the road would upset the barely balanced load on their applecart.

The bump came in the form of a tight job market for academic positions. Though Sonia's work had been outstanding, as she approached the end of her two-year fellowship, there were few tenured university positions open, and none of them interested her. For the first time in three years her spirits began to sink, and for extended periods her mood dropped as low as it had in her earlier depressive episodes.

This was a critical point in the marriage. Sonia was beginning to withdraw, and this threatened Jack's emotional stability. But since he knew that Sonia's unhappiness and seclusiveness had nothing to do with him, he was less likely to respond with his own depressed feelings. Likewise, it was important that Sonia keep her perspective, and take pains to reassure Jack that her low feelings related only to her career predicament, and not to him. She did what she could. Partly because she was so devoted to scientific rationality and partly because she was a depressive of the purely guilty variety, she could minimize the impact of her depression on Jack. She'd kept up with developments in neurochemistry (in her spare time), and could therefore explain her low moods to Jack in objective terms. Nonetheless, she couldn't avoid some degree of withdrawal from him. To Jack's credit, he did his best not to take this personally. But try as he might, her emotional unavailability made his spirits sink, and soon he too became depressed.

The timing could not have been worse—Jack was terribly depressed in the week or so before his play was to open, and his gloomy pessimism and leaden immobility took a toll on the last-minute preparations. He couldn't get out of bed in time to get to morning rehearsals, he couldn't concentrate well enough to make effective adjustments of sets and stagings, he was explosively irritable and bumbling and disorganized in directing the final few rehearsals—all direct consequences of his depression, but seen by the cast and others involved in the production as self-centered and misdirected anxiety about the success of his play. All this led to a number of problems on opening night, which in turn tarnished the success of the show over the course of its run. The director and cast, who understood nothing of Jack's eleventh-hour paralysis, felt betrayed and resentful.

Above and beyond the career crisis all this precipitated, Jack was now at a personal crisis. He'd never considered his moody temperament as anything but a matter of artistic style—and would never have imagined seeking treatment for it. He had always considered his temperament a thing apart from biological or biochemical factors—and, by extension, felt the same about Sonia. It would have been completely inconsistent with his sense of who he was to see his problems with mood or loneliness as a psychiatric disorder. To think this, he felt, would be to reduce his spirit and temperament to something mundane and spiritually neutral—like the color of his hair or the shape of his head. He could forgive himself, and Sonia, for the setback in his career, but he did not feel he could forgive himself for taking the easy (and inartistic) route of accepting a biochemical basis to his emotional reactions—as Sonia was now suggesting. He struggled with these issues for some time. Intellectual creature that he was, he knew that his identity as an artist and as a husband depended on whether he could share Sonia's view of mood and temperament to the point of accepting psychiatric treatment.

Jack's innate good sense and the extent of his academic and artistic success without the rewards of personal satisfaction (before meeting Sonia) clarified his priorities. He was a husband first and an artist second. He loved Sonia, and couldn't bear to watch her depression make her miserable. His artistic identity and career could not justify this. And he respected Sonia, and her intelligence, intuition, and logic. If she'd concluded that there was a biological basis to her temperament, and to his, then fine, he'd go along with that. Fortunately, Sonia's department head was an old friend of mine, and sent them to me for consultation.

Being Jack and Sonia, they spent the week or so before we met devouring the greater part of a fifteen-pound text on psychiatry, and could therefore characterize their predicament quite concisely in our first meeting. Jack, they'd concluded, was the type of depressive unusually sensitive to rejection, and would probably respond to a particular set of medications they suggested. Sonia, on the other hand, was more of a guilty depressive, most likely to respond to another set of medications. They also felt that couples therapy would be useful. I agreed, of course. Over the course of a few weeks the medications and the therapy were helpful to both of them, though it was a bit embarrassing to charge them for following their directions so obediently. I did, on the other hand, earn my fee over the next few months, because the practical tasks of helping the politically naive Jack put his career back together and Sonia persevere through the indignities of a job search took no small effort. So did the not so practical task of helping Jack continue to come to philosophical terms with the relationship of biochemistry to the intellect and spirit.

Between the medication and the talking therapy, Jack's sensitivity to rejection and Sonia's self-flagellating perfectionism diminished in the course of a few months. Jack was able to undo much of the damage to his career. His shyness disappeared almost completely, and he began lecturing on campus and giving readings from his poetry at bookstores around town. An academic position began to look likely for him—an inconceivable outcome only a few months before. Sonia was able to find a tenured position in another city that offered a number of opportunities for interesting research. The last I heard, both were pursuing academic careers at the new university with considerable success. Unfortunately, depression has continued to be a problem for Sonia in the unavoidable times when her work bogs down—apparently, as Jack suggested in a recent note, because her (prototypically professorial) absentmindedness makes her forget to take her medications much of the time. Fortunately, I have a colleague in their new town who promises to keep after her about this.

Paul and Melissa: The Perils of Polar Opposites

Clearly, biology was stacked against Jack and Sonia in their mutual susceptibility to depression. I chose their story, of course, because they did so well in keeping their depressive tendencies from sinking their relationship. They did this by tolerating their intellectual and temperamental differences well enough to share a significant degree of each other's attitudes, insights, and knowledge. It was especially useful for Jack to assimilate Sonia's scientific-mindedness as he came to terms with the nature of mood disorder. Opposites like Jack and Sonia often attract—what determines whether the attraction lasts is whether they're able to enrich themselves by sharing their differences, or whether they remain polarized, and contend or compete because of them. Our second couple, Paul and Melissa, are a pair of opposites whose substantial differences multiplied rather than mitigated their difficulties. Because of this, their mood disorders continually threatened their stability and ultimately ended their relationship.

Paul and Melissa were opposites in almost every way. Melissa was liveliness personified—pretty face, lilting voice alive with humor and innuendo, infectious laughter, boundless energy, enthusiasm, and enterprise, always moving, never at rest. Right from the start she was the center of attention in all she did, and, as far as anyone can recall, she never had a gloomy moment—until much later. In high school she had a dozen boyfriends all at the same time, but no one seemed to mind because Melissa had enough energy and enthusiasm for every one of them. Anyone stopping to wonder about Melissa might have noticed that behind her easy charm and social flexibility was an exaggerated need for everyone to like her—as if anyone's finding her less than delightful would mean that there was something wrong with her. A psychologically minded observer might have wondered if this need for approval represented a potential for depression, but no one ever worried about such a thing because Melissa was so charming and disarming, delightful and carefree. Clinically speaking, we'd have to say that Melissa's behavior was chronically and mildly hypomanic, but her thinking was never out of control and her behavior was never frenzied or inappropriate. Nor was there any sign of depression.

If Melissa was the incarnation of liveliness, Paul was the soul of sobriety. From his earliest days he was grimly precocious—walking early, talking early, reading early. Nothing he did, however, had the joy of adventure and conquest most bright children feel as they explore their world and exercise their talent. There was instead a sober goal-directedness—in school, in sports, in everything. His parents were concerned by the driven, joyless character of his life—but, being unsophisticated psychologically, they were easily consoled by teachers and school psychologists that all was well with Paul. Today we would be more concerned, but Paul had entered school just after the launch of Sputnik had shocked and sobered all America and especially its educational system. Youngsters like Paul were seen as the great American hope to catch up with the sudden and frightening superiority in space that Sputnik had given the Russians (with their pressure-cooker educational system and the coddling of their precocious students). In retrospect, though, Paul's gloomy and joyless march through childhood and adolescence was clearly symptomatic of a chronic depression.

It wasn't until they entered college that Paul and Melissa began to have overt psychiatric symptoms. If Melissa stayed up too late, drank too much, had too much excitement, or all three, her hypomania would escalate to a state of mild mania. Her mind would race, her activities would multiply, and her judgment would lag far behind. At other times, when she'd do poorly in class or didn't seem to be as popular as she'd like, her mood would drop. For a few days or a week she'd sleep late, stay home from class, and procrastinate on assignments. All this took a toll on her schoolwork and landed her on academic probation. The dean, fortunately a professor of psychology, recognized the pattern of mood swings and sent her to the counseling service, where the campus psychiatrist diagnosed cyclothymia. He carefully reviewed with Melissa the things she could do to get things back in control—get more sleep, stop drinking alcohol, try not to procrastinate, and so on. He also suggested a course of psychotherapy and a trial of medications to stabilize her mood swings. This intervention could have been very timely and very useful, but his vigor in presenting the diagnosis and in making his recommendations overwhelmed Melissa's capacity to listen to him. She left his office feeling demoralized and humiliated and, as if to verify her new diagnosis, took flight by dropping out of school for a semester. She took a job as a secretary in a law firm, enjoyed the liveliness (and the attention the male attorneys paid her), and decided after a few weeks to postpone college indefinitely.

Paul had enrolled at the same university, and had chosen the engineering school. Almost from the start he began to have periods of depression. During his first year they became more severe and lasted longer, and he soon began missing classes and falling behind on assignments. By what could have been a piece of good fortune, his academic adviser had had his own struggles with depression, recognized the condition in Paul, and gently suggested that he seek help at the campus health center. Unfortunately, Paul would have nothing to do with this advice. By sheer strength of will he pulled himself through each term—though the bouts of depression took a toll on his performance. Thus fortune, in an unusually benign spirit, had provided each Paul and Melissa the opportunity for an early intervention—but each in his own way squandered her offering.

Melissa knew that her life was going nowhere. She had taken the campus psychiatrist's advice more to heart than she'd realized, and had scaled down her life to avoid the excitement that she sensed could lead to manic or depressive mood swings. Thus her mood was stable, but her work and social life felt tedious and colorless.

In a similar way, Paul continued to fear his depressions—though outwardly he scoffed at the idea that they were serious. He knew that like Sonia's, his depressions followed times when he had trouble with his schoolwork, and therefore avoided courses that he feared were too hard for him. In this way he followed a path through the engineering school that was safe, but much less interesting than he would have preferred.

When Paul and Melissa met, then, each offered an attractive solution to the other's deepest fears. To Paul, life with Melissa promised a life of excitement that would make up for what looked to be a disappointingly unexciting career. He had never dated someone so attractive or exciting, and could not have imagined that there could be a dark side to her personality. To Melissa, Paul offered a rock-solid stability that would help maintain her equilibrium and prevent her mind from spinning out of control or sinking into despair. Paul, for example, cautioned Melissa about drinking, scolded her when she didn't get enough sleep, and so on. Neither, of course, could have admitted their motivations to themselves. They married at the beginning of Paul's last year at college.

The marriage worked well enough at first. After graduation, Paul took a job at a local engineering firm, and Melissa continued hers as a legal secretary. As long as Melissa was upbeat and enthusiastic, Paul's mood was stable; and as long as Paul was stable and supportive, Melissa's mood stayed upbeat. Nonetheless, the potential for trouble lurked just beneath the surface. Any drop in Melissa's hypomanic enthusiasm risked putting Paul face-to-face with his disappointment in himself and in his career. Any lapse in Paul's supportive and stabilizing influence risked Melissa's becoming manic or depressed. As with Jack and Sonia, then, a disruption in the relationship was inevitable, awaiting only a small bump in their marital path. And, like Jack and Sonia, whether it would topple the relationship would depend largely on how Paul and Melissa handled the consequences of whatever went wrong.

The inevitable came gradually. Typical of jobs in Silicon Valley,

Paul's work took over more and more of his time and energy. Melissa was disappointed at how little of Paul was left for her, and tried to react as she'd always reacted to disappointment— by keeping herself busy with a thousand simultaneous projects and activities. This time, however, it didn't work as well as it had in the past. Maybe she was older, she thought, or maybe she was just getting more resigned to life, but whatever the reason, during one especially long period in which Paul worked late every night and every weekend, Melissa's mood dropped precipitiously. She turned to Paul for comfort, but he didn't help. He was too tired from work, he said, and anyway, there's no point to being depressed—just pull yourself together. Buck up.

Paul's response, predictably enough, dropped Melissa's spirits even further. Her friends worried about her, and one, a patient of mine, insisted that she call me for an appointment. Unlike her response back in college, this time she followed the suggestion.

It was at this point that I learned most of what I've just written about Paul and Melissa. Melissa was indeed falling into a depression—her mood was down, her energy and enthusiasm were waning, her sleep and appetite were disrupted. The depression wasn't very severe, but it was getting worse by the day, and this frightened her. She'd never been this low before, and she didn't know how bad it might get. She knew that Paul's unavailability had precipitated the depression, and that his scolding her for it was making it worse—but she had no idea what a psychiatrist could do to help.

This was a critical point for Melissa. People seem to have their highest level of self-understanding when they're mildly depressed—neither manic denial nor depressive distortion obscures a realistic view of matters at hand, and the mild activation of the superego seems to add a productive intensity and courageous activity to self-observation. Thus, for the first time in her life, Melissa could see that she'd been on overdrive for decades. She was beginning to understand that her hypomanic style, and the depressive feelings hidden beneath it, had dominated all her life. It was thus an ideal time to come for professional help. We reviewed her life, her personality style, and her marriage, and how she wanted them to change. I explained what I could of the psychological and biological factors at work, and how they'd conspired to make her life what it was. She was receptive to what I said, and agreed to a course of psychotherapy and a trial of medication. She also wanted Paul to join us for the first few sessions.

Paul's response could not have been more different from Jack's (which is why I've chosen him for this example, of course). He had little interest in the details of what Melissa was experiencing and what she wanted from him. She needed to snap out of this nonsense, he said, and be her old self. Besides, he went on, this sort of thing (psychiatry) was just a crutch—medication especially. It was the easy way out. I tried to appeal to his scientific inclinations. Had he heard or read about medication? No, he hadn't. Did he know what we've learned in the last four or five decades about the ways the brain works? No, he didn't. Was he interested in learning something about these things? Not really. Could he see how much his attitude was upsetting his wife? That was ridiculous—Melissa (who was crying as he spoke) was a strong woman and didn't need a lot of overpriced coddling from someone like me. Had he ever experienced anything like Melissa was going through now? Of course not.

It would have made things worse if I'd pressed Paul about his resistance to what Melissa was hoping to do in treatment. We left it alone, and didn't invite Paul back to our sessions. Melissa's mood lifted back to its hypomanic baseline over the course of a few weeks. Not so surprisingly, she soon reported that Paul's mood was beginning to drop, but that he wouldn't consider treatment. Melissa began to fear that the marriage could not absorb the growth she hoped to attain, and Paul soon removed any doubt about the matter. As he became more and more depressed, he took up with his nineteen-year-old secretary (a mindless little hypomanic, Melissa called her), and moved in with her about two months into Melissa's treatment. Fortunately, she'd been bracing herself for this eventuality for some time, and quickly gained perspective on what was happening—and filed for divorce. Over the next few years she returned to college and, at last report, was on her way toward a career in theater arts, and was engaged to a professor of drama. I've lost track of Paul altogether.

How Not to Be Paul and Melissa

There are two things you'll each need to do to know if your relationship is being ambushed by a psychiatric disorder. The first is to maintain an appropriate mind-set toward problems that seem to pop up out of nowhere. The second is to know something about the common psychiatric syndromes—the devil you know being easier to deal with than the one you don't know. And these disorders can be demonic.

The Mind-set: Stop, Drop, and Roll

If your clothes catch fire, we all tell our kids, you stop, drop, and roll. I tell grown-ups to do the same sort of things when a relationship starts going up in smoke: *Stop* (before you retaliate, run away, and so on), *think* (there must be some reason for this, including the emergence of a psychiatric disorder), and last, *role review* (review whether you're doing something to make all this happen, or to keep it from getting better). This isn't easy—it's more natural to respond first and think later. But whether you're the partner or the one ambushed by the disorder, if you don't stop and wonder about what you're dealing with, you can't do much about it. Fine, but how exactly do you do all this?

How to Recognize if the Problem Is a Psychiatric Disorder

First (as usual), you have to be familiar with the syndromes likely to ambush a relationship. Let's say your partner is becoming irritable and even abusive; is this a depression, an irritable mania, PMS? If you suspect a particular disorder, then ask yourself about the other symptoms. Is your newly irritable partner waking in the middle of the night, barraging himself with self-reproach, losing interest in sex, or showing other signs of depression? Is he talking faster, sleeping less, starting a million projects at once, or showing other signs of mania?

If your partner is becoming more scattered or disorganized, could it be an exacerbation of ADD? In this case, you have to think about whether he's always been this way—that is, impulsive, inattentive, and otherwise typical of a person with ADD. If your partner is getting hypersexual or outright promiscuous, you have to think about hypomania or mania, and ask yourself the standard questions about bipolar disorder. Likewise, if he's acting secretive, or much more fearful, you have to wonder if OCD, panic disorder, or a phobia is emerging, and review the relevant symptoms. All this may at first sound tedious or complicated, but it isn't really. There are only a few major conditions that cause the most trouble, and each has only a few symptoms and diagnostic hints associated with it. And considering how important it is to identify these disorders, the work involved to run down the list of disorders and the symptoms (or to reread parts of Chapters Two through Four) is surely worth the effort.

It is possible, on the other hand, that after you review the syndromes, none seems to apply. In that case, your partner may be acting up without suffering from a psychiatric disorder. As I've said all along, though this book is about the effect of psychiatric disorders, there's a lot of mischief in relationships that has nothing to do with psychiatric disorders. People in midlife who are trying to deny their loss of youth, for example, can be promiscuous or jump into shaky business ventures without a trace of mania—they're simply acting out their vanity and immaturity. Nonetheless, a partner deserves the benefit of the doubt before you decide he's acting up just because he's a jerk. It's also possible that he is suffering from a psychiatric disorder, but that you're missing it. Psychiatric consultation can be useful in ruling this out.

A second set of factors that help identify an emerging psychiatric disorder are specific precipitants. Loss, as we've established, commonly precipitates manic or depressive episodes. Thus, if you're wondering if your partner is acting up because he's depressed, ask yourself if he's recently lost someone or something valuable. This includes abstract or symbolic losses like the loss of prestige after a demotion at work, or of the excitement of organizing a project when it's completed. If your partner seems to be having a sudden increase of his ADD symptoms, think whether life has gotten more complicated recently (was it the new baby, the new promotion, the new deadline for his project?). For PTSD and phobias, naturally enough, you'll have to look for trauma, recent or remote. What provokes OCD or GAD is generally less clear, but almost any situation that adds stress and complexity can do this.

A third factor is periodicity. The most familiar example, of course, is PMS. Is she trouble for only a few days each month, and delightful otherwise? Is she tearful, gloomy, irritable, or unapproachable only then? Does it get worse year by year? Wait until the stormy days have passed before raising this issue aloud. Most women won't appreciate your raising the matter when they're in the middle of it. Besides, since mood affects thinking so powerfully, she won't be as clear about anything, her mood included, during the PMS time as she is when it's over. Bipolar disorders have their own periodicity, sometimes recurring at a particular time of year, occasionally even to the day. For many people, depression is more common in winter, and manic episodes are more common in fall and spring.

A fourth factor is especially palpable—an increase in blaming, especially with the onset of a mood disorder. In good relations and during good times, issues of blame arise infrequently, if at all. If something goes wrong, each partner works to get things back in order rather than to blame anyone for it. At these times, the question of who caused the problem matters only if it helps identify how things went wrong in order to prevent it happening again. When someone's depressed, on the other hand, the tendency to self-criticism escalates. A depressed person will either blame himself, often completely irrationally—or, if he can't bear the guilt this generates, he'll pass it off to someone else. A partner, unfortunately, is a favorite target. Manics almost *always* blame somebody else for the havoc they wreak because, after all, there's nothing whatever wrong with them.

What to do

Practical details of getting professional help are covered in Chapter Eleven. Here I'll address some of the more personal and psychological issues involved. I chose partners for our examples who were nearly polar opposites because this makes a couple's response to an emerging psychiatric problem especially visible. The determining moment for each couple occurred when one partner learned that the other had a psychiatric problem. How Jack and Paul reacted depended on how well they had assimilated the differences between themselves and their wives all along. How they reacted in crisis, then, was an intensified version of their usual style. Jack's assimilation of what was different in Sonia enriched his experience all along, and at the point of crisis helped him accept the biological foundation of Sonia's depression. Because of this he could respond to her realistically and helpfully. Paul, on the other hand, all along had used their differences self-servingly—he'd relied on Melissa's hypomanic exuberance to distract himself from the feelings of depression he wanted to deny. Thus at his point of crisis he wasn't able to consider Melissa's needs as important as his own. Instead of tending to her emotional pain, he complained about it—her mood was no longer useful to him.

The examples show that when psychiatric problems emerge, overt and hidden differences and similarities in partners' temperaments and vulnerabilities to painful emotions (depression, anxiety, and so on) are crucial. They determine how well each can respond to the other's difficulties. Thus, if you find that you can't cope with these feelings in your partner, it's possible that you share his feelings and vulnerabilities, but that you've hidden them away (for fear of their overwhelming you). As our cases show, this circumstance is especially thorny with the emergence of mood or anxiety disorders.

Thus, if your partner becomes depressed, for example, and you can't comfort him, you need to ask yourself at least two questions. First, is depression part of your own makeup, and is his depression starting to activitate yours (like Jack and Sonia)? Second, are you intolerant of his depression because you've been relying on his good moods to sustain yours (like Paul with Melissa)? Or, if your partner becomes excessively anxious or phobic and you can't tolerate it, ask yourself whether he's activating similar fears and anxieties in you. Likewise, if you can't be supportive to a partner struggling with the onset of OCD, you have to wonder whether your own issues about perfectionism or compulsivity (or maybe even OCD) are being activated.

* * *

As I've said before, it's important to keep in mind that psychiatric disorders are only one of the things that can ambush a relationship. The problem of hidden similarities, for example, applies to situations without major psychiatric problems—after all, everyone hates in others what we hate (and deny) in ourselves. Sometimes the problems are simpler than the psychological and psychiatric processes I've been describing. All of us can simply be selfish or ignorant or lazy, and don't care or know or attend to the fact that in times of distress, a partner needs a good deal of attention and understanding, and that withholding our time or energy or caring at such times is abusive, whatever our motivation or excuse.

On the other hand, if you're having trouble being caring and attentive to a partner with a psychiatric disorder, it may be that it isn't from selfishness, ignorance, or laziness. After all, people with these disorders are hard to deal with. Nonetheless, you owe it to your partner to do your best—including expending the effort and kindness to ask the sort of questions I've just listed.

Most of what I've discussed so far are obstacles to helping a partner in distress. As usual, once the obstacles are removed, most people can respond reasonably. This involves getting appropriate help as soon as possible. At the same time, it helps to let your partner know explicitly that you understand that his symptoms are not in his control, and that you're not going to ridicule, disdain, or abandon him because of them. He may not be able to believe this, but he needs to hear it, usually repeatedly. You also have to listen. What I said in Chapter Three about men dealing with depressed women applies to all the disorders and to all men and women. We men have the tendency to jump in too fast and try to fix things without listening carefully enough to what those things might be. People have a strong need to talk about their emotional distress—for a number of reasons. For one thing, someone listening to them reassures them that what they're going through isn't bizarre, repugnant, or otherwise unacceptable, and won't automatically lead to disdain and rejection. They also need to hear themselves out loud. This helps them reflect on what they're saying and therefore begin to get it into perspective. Being listened to by someone we love at a time when we're suffering is the adult counterpart to a sad or frightened child being held and comforted by a loving parent. Listening to your partner without judgment or complaint offers this comfort, and can go a long way toward making the worst of experiences tolerable enough to let him begin to heal.

CHAPTER 7

How Your Brain Can Keep You Out of Relationships Altogether

There are millions of people who go through life never knowing the comforts and security of a lasting relationship, and there are a million reasons for this. Fortunately, a great many of these people can be helped substantially, sometimes without a great expenditure of time or energy. This makes identifying them terribly important. How to do so is the theme of this chapter.

As I said at the end of the last chapter, psychiatric disorders can make a person hard to live with, sometimes to the point that relationships simply don't work for him. As we've seen, it's especially hard to deal with a depressed person. He's the proverbial porcupine—his neediness makes his conversation tedious and his interest in others minimal. His irritability makes him prickly, and his self-preoccupation and faultfinding depress or exasperate anyone who tries to get close to him. All this leads to the irony that the person who needs companionship the most rejects it the most vigorously.

Nonetheless, these particular porcupines can be diagnosed (as depressed) and treated—and thereby lose their quills. The same is true for people with the other disorders. What makes diagnosing them difficult is that they have symptoms that look more like personality traits than like entries on a symptom list. Because of this, no one, including potential partners or even therapists, can tell at first glance that they actually have treatable conditions—and only look like porcupines. Their personalities mimic a number of thorny, and nearly untreatable, psychiatric conditions. Their symptoms and character traits are so problematical that they're most often incapable of ongoing relationships.

The people who really do have personality problems and other disorders that are very hard to treat or endure I'll call the Real Impossibles. They in turn are composed of three subgroups I'll call the very unusual, the very unruly, and the very neurotic. I'll contrast them with the three groups that mimic them—and who at first seem just as impossible as the real items.

This may all sound convoluted, but the diagram below shows that the classification is pretty simple. I'll explain how the mimics of the impossibles can simulate actual impossibility so well, and give some ways to determine if someone you know, or maybe even you, fit into the groups of pseudo-impossibility.

The Impossibles

I. The Real Impossibles

The very unusual   The very unruly   The very neurotic

II. The Mimics of the Impossibles

Mimics of the unusual   Mimics of the unruly   Mimics of the neurotic

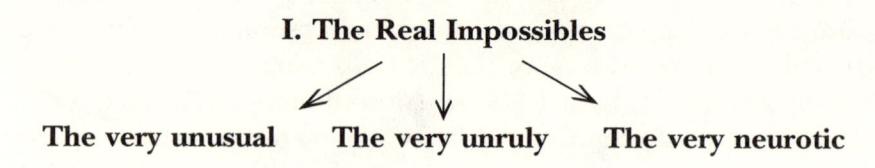

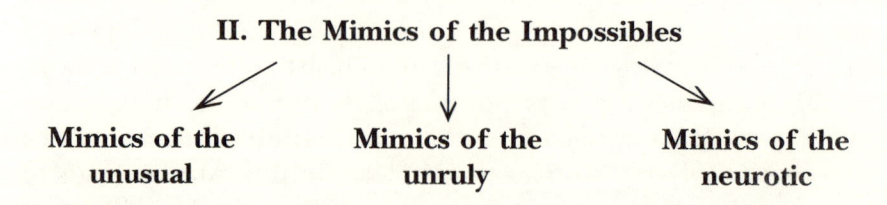

Like greatness, Real Impossibility is sometimes born, and sometimes attained. That is, the Real Impossibles are a mixed group both in their characteristics (very unusual, very unruly, or very neurotic), and in what has made them this way. As far as we

know, someone becomes Impossible either from a set of unusually traumatic experiences in childhood, or from built-in biochemical abnormalities. Or it can be both—since these conditions are probably inheritable, parents of Impossible children are likely to be Impossible themselves, and tend, therefore, to traumatize their children.

We know more about traumatic causes than those that are inborn. For many children, even those with no susceptibility to major mental disorders, interpersonal life is so painful, barren, or confusing that they don't learn how to relate to others comfortably. Children devise ways to get through difficult times and, if the times are difficult enough, they cling to those ways throughout life—no matter how much experience shows them that they don't work anymore. Because children's minds are still developing, troubling experiences and troublesome responses to them are programmed so deeply that they persist throughout life and are very resistant to treatment. As every pet owner knows, the same thing happens with cats, dogs, and other animals. In fact, the story of one strangely human kitty captures this process surprisingly well. His story provides a more concise example than I can imagine from anyone in our own species.

The mother of the little black kitten in question was, aside from a few training analysts I've met, the crabbiest, most irascible creature imaginable, a scruffy, yellow-tan bundle of bad attitude. This mother would box and batter her kittens, sit on them, pounce on them, worry and torment them whenever she was feeling mean—which was whenever she was awake. Over time they learned to give her space, and when she'd come home after spreading a little misery around the neighborhood, they'd scurry away like a litter of tumbleweeds in a sandstorm.

When the little victims were about six months old, some misguided person stole Spot. The effect on her babies was wondrous; they cuddled up to me and to my other cat, Mehitabel, as if we were their natural mother. We were flattered, and our offspring prospered, especially the little black one, who in a matter of months grew so big, we had to call him Thor. He was, as his water dish proclaimed, the LORD OF THE NEIGHBORHOOD—until one dark day when a scruffy-looking yellow-tan cat strolled into the neighborhood. Barely a third his bulk, she walked straight up to him, thinking, one has to imagine, that one should make friends with someone of Thor's stature. Thor, however, took barely a moment's glance, pointed himself north, and shot off, all thirty-something pounds of him, at about Mach III, never to be seen or heard from again.

Thus, having been traumatized in childhood, Thor spent his life hiding from any frightening encounter, especially females who reminded him of his mother. Spot's antisocial personality was also the product of childhood trauma. Naming her, a kitten of all one (scuzzy yellow) color, Spot struck her (one imagines) as singularly unempathic of her owners—and left a tender spot in her psyche and a twist in her personality to protest it (she never realized that the idea was that she, Spot, was the spot).

We know less about the purely *inborn* causes of the real Impossible conditions. There are almost certainly neurochemical abnormalities in all of them. Research shows this with varying degrees of certainty for different conditions—the clearest with schizophrenia and probably least with the character disorders (see below). As in any field, where the data is scarce, controversy is abundant—and best for us to avoid. Whatever the ultimate causes of Real Impossibility, the most important fact for us is that they're difficult to treat, especially compared to the conditions that mimic them. The image of an animal psychologist sprinting madly after Thor at Mach III, reviewing his childhood and urging him to get in touch with his feelings about his mother—this captures something of the futility of the effort. Likewise, we've all learned that treating someone like Spot is a study in exasperation (if not laceration). Most therapists have been worn out by futile adventures like these many times (usually early in our careers when we didn't know better).

Thus doctors and laymen alike come to view the Thors of our experience as peculiar and the Spots as unruly, and avoid them or incarcerate them. The irony is that corresponding to the Thors and the Spots are a number of social phobics or depressives or people with OCD (and so on) who mimic their peculiarity or unruliness, but who can be treated like any other phobic, depressive, or person with OCD. It's a shame that there are many psychiatrists and other therapists who don't know about this, or dismiss it as simplistic or naive without thinking through the issues involved. I will explain, largely by example, the differences between the truly Impossible Spots and Thors of our species and their mimics—who, unless they're properly identified and treated, are likely to spend their lives shut out from ongoing human relationships.

I'll start with the most puzzling group—the very unusual and their mimics.

Very Unusual People—and Their Mimics

People in these groups seem odd in appearance, speech, manners, or mannerisms. They may be withdrawn or inappropriately chatty, nearly immobile or aimlessly restless, coldly unemotional or emotionally explosive. Whatever the pattern of their conduct or appearance, they seem to be out of step with other people. These are the loners we see wandering the streets but never speaking to anyone, at jobs without much human contact, or in institutions, whether in halfway houses, jails, or other places for people who don't fit into society. They're the ones behind counters at out of the way shops who don't return your greeting or look away before you can offer it. Or who accost you in parks or town centers, and in too loud voices and with too exaggerated expressions and gestures preach ideas at you that don't make much sense. It's difficult to imagine any of them in a lasting relationship.

This group makes up a surprisingly large part of the population. Adding up estimates for the various subgroups, it seems they make up from three to five percent of the population.

The most impaired subgroup is that of autism. Typically, there is little or no interest or understanding of others and a limited capacity to communicate. In severe cases, a person has no investment at all in other people. Behavior may be bizarrely repetitive and idiosyncratic. Autistic people strike others as strangely mechanical and impossible to reach in any personal way. Dustin Hoffman played a mildly impaired autistic person in the movie *Rain Man*. Fortunately, the syndrome is rare, accounting for two to five people per ten thousand.

Another severely impaired group are people with schizophrenia. Schizophrenia is not rare—it represents about one percent of the population. Unlike people with autism, schizophrenics do relate to others, but their relations are severely limited by difficulties with thought, emotion, and activity. They're commonly troubled by hallucinations, usually of voices talking to them or about them. Their thoughts are chaotic, illogical, or delusional. Delusional thinking involves fixed ideas or systems of ideas that a person will not set aside in the face of clear evidence refuting them. With no evidence, for example, a person may believe that his neighbors are plotting to humiliate or kill him. Or he may believe that serpents are digesting his liver or that worms are swimming in his brain. His speech can be disjointed or otherwise peculiar and, at worst, is useless for conveying information. Activity may be chaotic or almost absent. Any or all of this may come and go over time, but when present, the symptoms are disastrous to relationships.

Although schizophrenia cannot be cured, there are many whose symptoms are controlled almost completely with medication. The remainder suffer from persistent symptoms despite taking medication. Even when the symptoms come under control, difficulties relating to others tend to persist and disrupt chances for having long-term relationships.

Schizophrenia itself isn't usually mimicked by people with more easily treated disorders, but rather by three conditions that resemble schizophrenia, though without overt psychotic symptoms. These are the schizoid, schizotypal, and paranoid personalities. A schizoid person is the consummate loner. He has little if any interest in people or what they do. He doesn't desire or enjoy relationships, is indifferent to praise or criticism, shows little emotion, and has no friends or confidants except for family members. The prevalence is not known. A schizotypal person looks much like a schizophrenic but does not experience the overt hallucinations, delusions, or fragmentation of thought and behavior that characterize schizophrenia. His thoughts, behavior, and speech, however, are peculiar or eccentric. He is uncomfortable with close relationships, and has little capacity for them. Schizotypal people are thought to represent around three percent of the population. A paranoid personality is distrustful and suspicious, and feels, without basis, that others mean him harm or are trying to deceive him—but, unlike a schizophrenic, he doesn't have overt hallucinations or unshakable delusions. He bears grudges, finds demeaning or threatening remarks or actions that are truly benign, and is preoccupied with unjustified doubts about the loyalty or trustworthiness of anyone he associates with. The prevalence of this disorder is estimated to be between .5 percent and 2.5 percent of the population.

Treating people with autism or one of the schizophrenialike personality disorders is enormously difficult. It's costly, time-consuming, and often not very successful. Psychiatrists must settle for managing these conditions, like internists or neurologists managing incurable conditions like diabetes or Parkinson's disease.

The group of mimics, however, are very treatable, and this is why they're so important to identify. Almost any of the more treatable disorders can mimic the less treatable ones. For example, a person with agoraphobia or with severe ADD may be unsociable and withdrawn, have few friends or acquaintances, and take a job working alone or at night (or both). In this way he looks like a withdrawn schizoid who typically gravitates to living alone, working alone, and so on. Once we look beneath the symptoms, however, the difference is tremendous. The agoraphobic is simply frightened of being out of his house or familiar workplace, the person with ADD is overwhelmed by interpersonal stimulation and must hide away to avoid it. Neither of them has the schizoid's utter disregard for human opinion or companionship, the schizotypal's peculiarity, or the paranoid's suspiciousness.

In the same way, someone with severe OCD can be so tormented by obsessions or compulsions that the senseless preoccupation, bizarre rituals, and resulting seclusiveness can look schizotypal or even schizophrenic. A depressed person too can be so withdrawn and fearful that he looks schizoid, or, if the depression reaches the point of delusions, like a schizophrenic. A manic too can become so psychotic that at least during an episode, can be indistinguishable from a schizophrenic.

There's a common emotional denominator to the mimics that makes identification much easier. This is their exaggerated emotional sensitivity—exactly the opposite of the isolated autistic, schizoid, or schizotypal person, who's generally oblivious of interpersonal influence (especially for the first two groups). Right from the cradle things hurt the mimics more than other children. Loud noises, falls off bicycles, scoldings—things that roll off more kids make one of these children close up like a turtle. Over time, sadly enough, the sensitivity takes its toll. I've seen perfectly cheerful toddlers get more and more timid, shy, and ultimately gloomy as the pain and humiliation they feel from ordinary rejections and indignities wear down their high spirits. Their self-confidence erodes as they learn they can't protect themselves from other children hurting them, and, since most children can't resist tormenting kids they know are vulnerable, things get worse as time goes on. Their enthusiasm for playing with other kids drains away as they learn that sooner or later someone's going to hurt their feelings or laugh at them. With time they retreat within themselves because they can't bear this. It's sad to watch. Fortunately, we're learning to treat these children, and it seems that the earlier they're treated, the less sensitive they'll be later on.

As I've insisted all along, the conditions I'm calling mimics of the unusual are treatable, often to the point of complete remission. The challenge is to identify the mimics, and get them to treatment. In my experience, the mimics of the unusual groups are among the easiest to get into treatment. They've suffered and been misunderstood so long—being called strange or odd or weird—that learning about their condition and that it's treatable is a great relief. Their shyness is an obstacle, but if the person who's told them about the possibility for help goes along, they usually go willingly.

The most vivid example I've seen of the mimicry of one of the unusual disorders was my first—a strange old woman who puzzled me so much that I'm sure she helped propel me into psychiatry. I was barely twenty, and, as usual, nearly out of money. My girlfriend and I decided to save what little we had by sharing lunch at the dorm. Halfway through the line we ran headlong into the glare of a hard-looking gray-haired old woman who was assaulting the dining room floor with mop and bucket.

"You're sharing your food?!" she creaked with such scorn and condemnation that we felt as if we'd stolen it from an orphanage. Having fixed us with her icy glare, she went on.

"You must have rocks in your head."

What on earth was she talking about? I was as intrigued as if I'd seen Jonah (or his whale) climb out of the old scrub bucket. Who was this woman? Did she really say that? Why?

I hate it when I don't understand something, and having had no idea what would make someone talk like that, I puzzled over it for years. Over time, her quip became a sort of yardstick for my growth into a psychiatrist. In my Freudian days I thought I'd caught some meaning in her "rocks in your head" comment as a grudging complaint that organs other than my brain were guiding my behavior. Later, when I'd learned about personality disorders, I imagined that she was autistic or schizoid, and without any regard for what we might think, had said the first thing that popped into her head. But that couldn't have been it—she did care about us, if only to disdain and scold us. Was she schizophrenic and imagining that there was some danger to our sharing food? No, that wasn't it; I'd watched her for months after our encounter, and she didn't have the peculiarity or disorganization you spot so quickly in schizophrenics after working with them a few years.

By the time I'd finished my psychiatric training, I'd seen my share of autistic and schizophrenic and schizophrenic-like patients, and I couldn't imagine any of them acting like her. I'd decided by then that she was probably a depressive, most likely a chronic depressive for whom life had brought little comfort or companionship. There may have been trauma in her childhood, depressives are miserable, with or without help from their parents, abusive or otherwise. And if they suffer long enough, they learn to protect themselves in ways that can look quite strange. They become aloof, for example, convinced they don't need anyone because other people are inferior or uninteresting. Or they become cantankerous or sadistic or bizarre and drive others away before the others can drive them away—something they feel deep down will happen whenever they meet someone. Then again, they might suppress their feelings altogether, and act and feel like automata. In any of these ways they become what I've called mimics of the unusual. It seemed to me that our woman of the kitchen did all these maneuvers and probably many more.

But I still didn't know—and I hate that. Something on the drive back to California after my residency brought her to mind and brought me to an outlandish idea—it would be only about five hundred miles out of the way to get back to that dormitory and see if I could find someone to ask about her. Someone who remembered her must be around, I convinced myself. Maybe this way I could learn once and for all what was so wrong with that woman. After all, five hundred miles wasn't so far to go for something I'd wondered about for fifteen years. That's only thirty-three miles a year, I reasoned, and headed back to my old campus.

When I got there, I did find someone who remembered her (she'd died some eight years before). One of the cooks, himself about to retire, had known her since grade school. He said she'd been a relatively normal youngster until around the end of high school. She'd been a shy kid, sometimes gloomy, and pessimistic, he recalled, but probably not much more than lots of other teenagers. She'd had a twin brother. They'd been close and shared everything—friends, hobbies, homework. But in the last year of school he drowned in a boating accident. Only a last-minute change of plans kept her from being on the same boat and drowning along with her brother. She never recovered from the loss. For months she cried continually, thought about her brother constantly, and year by year became more and more depressed about losing him. Gradually she withdrew from everyone, and lived alone.

As time went by, she became more aloof than withdrawn, and rarely spoke to other people. In the thirty years they'd worked together, she'd hardly said a word to the cook. What I remembered of her was typical only of her last years, he said. In those years she was bothered by arthritis and other nagging ailments that added a bitterness to her reclusiveness. At times and with certain people (and with a long series of Saint Bernards) she could set aside her crabbiness and be somewhat kind and personable. Still, he'd always thought it would have been better had she drowned along with her brother—and he thought that she'd felt the same way.

* * *

Could a doctor, armed with the treatments now available, have treated this woman after the accident and softened its effect on her emotional life? I think so. The loss of a sibling is devastating and it's worse when it's a twin. Nonetheless, most people recover their equilibrium after a period of mourning, and reconnect with the world of things and people, and move on emotionally. From what I've seen, without a predisposition to depression, a person doesn't build walls of peculiarity and contempt like our old woman did for the last forty years of her life. Even with a predisposition to depression, though, I think her life could have been very different if a therapist had been available to help and to treat the depression medically. By the time I met her, though, it may well have been too late. It's hard to imagine breaking through that crusty exterior, even if you had the tact, patience, and psychiatric medication necessary.

But it may not have been too late. I wouldn't have imagined George Balusteri changing very much, but he did, and in a very short time. My pessimism about treating our old fussbudget stems from how difficult psychological treatment can be with patients like her, even after the biological component is treated. It takes a long time to win the trust of someone like her, and longer still to work through all the layers of defensiveness. But, as George's experience shows, if the problems are based on a biological disorder, in the best of times treating it can facilitate a surprisingly good resolution of the psychological problems—sometimes with little or no formal psychotherapy (and sometimes with a lot). We'll never know about her, but examples like hers and George's—with a much better outcome when treatment is available—mean that we must identify people like them, and do our best to treat them.

Very Unruly People—and Their Mimics

Beyond the occasional sniping and irritability by mimics like our depressive-turned-fussbudget, most unusual people have the decency to mind their own business—too much so, in fact, and that's their problem. The group I'm calling the very unruly, on the other hand, can't keep out of other people's business. They make their problems everyone else's problems and that's the trouble with them. Each in his own way leaves a trail of debris (both real and imaginary), confusion, and disillusionment. These are the ultimate incorrigibles, the sort who give us nightmares about sending our children out into the world. Their defining characteristic is an almost complete lack of conscience, making them a very nasty group. They're the ones who'll pick a fight in a grocery line because they're bored, dump over your shopping cart if you ignore the provocation, and then go off, get drunk, and laugh about the look on your face. They're the bikers who trash your car, fondle your girlfriend, and beat you up because they don't like your looks. They're the con men who swindle your grandmother out of her life savings, or, if they're attractive, con you into a one-night stand to steal your wallet, or molest your children, and then vanish without a trace or a second thought. They're the hit men and assassins who'll kill you with no questions asked (beyond the size of the payoff). Sometimes they're brighter or more sophisticated, but no less toxic—like the corporate pirate who takes over and then destroys a company, putting thousands of people out of work because he stands to make a killing, so to speak. And on and on.

There are several subgroups of unruly people, each with its own list of unendearing characteristics. The antisocial personality is the prototypic con artist. He has a bland disregard for the rights of others, and is therefore exploitative, deceitful, and irresponsible, without a shred of remorse for the havoc he wreaks on other people's lives. Close relationships are out of the question for him; his lack of regard for others is so complete that the very idea would amuse him.

The borderline personality is the poster child for instability—of mood, self-image, emotion, behavior, or (especially) relationships. Borderline personalities routinely abuse drugs as well as themselves and others. The borderline cannot stand being alone, and will do anything to keep others nearby, but persisting relationships are very unlikely in the midst of all this instability.

The histrionic personality combines the instability of the borderline with the neediness of the depressive, resulting in excessive, if shallow, emotionality and attention seeking. These traits make emotional give-and-take with others unlikely and predispose him to a childlike role in any relationship. Since he demands to be the center of attention, partners quickly tire of the role of admiring onlooker, and move on.

The narcissistic personality is preoccupied with maintaining an image of superiority. Even more than the histrionic, he's obsessed with being admired. He nonetheless holds himself aloof from others, approaching them only to extract whatever admiration they may show him. Once he attains it, he tosses them off with the nonchalance of a spider discarding the carcass of a fly whose life juices he's just sucked dry.

Collectively, this is a chilling group, best handled by staying away. That they don't form lasting relationships almost goes without saying. Treating them is usually an exercise in stupidity and self-abuse, although there are times when the patience of an oak tree and the skill of a neurosurgeon do produce improvement in a patient from one of these groups. Much more important for us, though, is that the group of mimics of the unrulies can be treated, often with dramatic improvement. It may be that in time all the unruly people will be treatable—as we uncover treatable biochemical abnormalities underlying the tangled thinking, unregulated aggression, and deficient self-control that characterize the group. At present, at least, we know enough to identify a number of treatable mimics.

ADD can mimic these conditions in a number of ways. As we saw in Chapter Two, a lifetime of failure to understand, perform, or communicate like people without ADD often leads to frustration and demoralization. Over time these develop into resentment, sometimes vindictiveness, and often into an unruly vengefulness bordering on psychopathic. This can be complicated by an attempt to self-medicate with stimulants. In some cases, it leads to an addiction to these substances, with all the antisocial behavior that goes with that territory.

Though I've said that addiction is too broad a topic to cover in this book, it's important to mention it. Addiction to any number of substances can lead to unruly behavior, especially in the context of a psychiatric disorder. People with phobias, panic attacks, GAD, or PTSD, for example, often try to control their symptoms with alcohol. Likewise, people who are depressed try to cheer themselves up with alcohol, speed, or cocaine, and people who are manic try to take the edge off their frenzied highs with alcohol or else boost their spirits on the downside of a high with stimulants. All this can lead to addictions mimicking the unruly behavior or borderline, histrionic, and antisocial personalities.

Depression is the other great mimic. The chronic depressive's low self-esteem and lack of interest in the world can simulate a narcissistic personality with its preoccupation with sources of self-esteem. I've seen patients whose self-involvement and disregard for others' welfare made them look like textbook examples of narcissistic personality—only to see the pathology melt away with antidepressant treatment and reveal perfectly kind and empathic people hidden under the icy exterior of narcissistic character armor. If he's attractive, or talented enough, a chronic depressive's low self-esteem can also lead him to frenzied plays for the attention and flattery he imagines will boost his self-esteem, making him look for all the world like a histrionic personality.

The most important practical task here is having the presence of mind to think of mimicry in the face of the abuse these people can heap on you. Then you can use the symptom lists and other diagnostic hints. If a person seems unruly because of an exaggerated need for admiration, for example, think depression or ADD. If a person is terribly fickle or wildly promiscuous, think mania or ADD. If a person is preoccupied with himself, and unusually resentful of anyone who isn't, think depression. If a person seems like all of the above, or doesn't follow any of the usual patterns, think alcohol, cocaine, speed, and so on. As usual, any change from usual behavior is a red flag. Personality disorders begin during childhood, whereas addictions and most of the psychiatric conditions (except ADD) begin in adolescence or adulthood.

Members of the unruly groups aren't going to listen to you very well—if at all. Unfortunately, this sometimes includes the mimics. If they were the type to listen to reason, they probably would have mimicked something less unruly—like a neurosis (see next section). Probably the best way to help them is arm in arm with the authorities. If, for example, your husband has been abusing you, never pays his bills, and runs off with five women at a time, you (or your attorney) may be able to convince an enlightened judge to get him treated for bipolar disorder, ADD, or alcohol or stimulant abuse. Sometimes you may have to be the authority. Anyone who's raised a child will recognize that what I'm saying is that the unruly, real or mimics, are overgrown two- or three-year-old children who need limits imposed by grown-ups. With this group, then, you'll need to exert some parental authority as you would for any other two- or three-year-old. If your spouse, for example, is so desperate to look good that he's bankrupted you buying clothes and jewelry, or driven you to distraction over endless flirations and trysts, you may have to insist he be evaluated and treated for depression or dysthymia before you let him spend any more money. As usual, I use "him" to mean "him or her" to emphasize that whether husband or wife, someone like this is rarely the family breadwinner—and to underscore that both men and women can be histrionic personalites, real or mimic.

Very Neurotic People—and Their Mimics

Neurotics are a group, first popularized by Freud, whose experiences with their parents created a set of persisting emotional problems. These are the prototypes of purely psychological problems—no help from biology is needed. Generally neurotics are much better at relationships than any of the personalities we've discussed so far. It can happen, though, that a particularly thorny set of neurotic problems prevents a person from forming relationships—as well as from doing well in psychotherapy intended to unravel the problems.

A typical example of the development and persistence of a neurosis involves a little girl I'll call Carol. We'll suppose she's extremely attached to her father, and therefore competitive with her mother over him—yet at the same time overly dependent on her. Trouble comes when her wish to spend all her time with her father upsets her mother, who herself is competitive with her daughter over the father. Since Carol is both dependent on her mother for emotional support and hostile toward her over the competition for her father, she's got a conflict. If she tries to spend a lot of time with her father, she risks losing her mother's emotional support. On the other hand, if she tries to placate her mother by spending less time with her father, she feels bad because she misses him and because she feels defeated by her mother.

We all go through something like this in childhood. We all had parents or other caretakers whom we overidealized as either very good or very bad, felt competitive with one or the other or both, tried to ally with one against the other, felt ganged up on by both, or had any of a hundred other standard child-parent conflicts that kids must somehow negotiate.

Freud called this set of conflicts the Oedipus complex (after the mythological king of Thebes who, not knowing the identity of his parents, killed his father and married his mother). They're the basis of what poets call the eternal triangle—the latter-day echoes of the early child-parent struggles. The Oedipal issues and conflicts seem most intense between four and six years of age, recede during late childhood, and re-emerge in adolescence to be repeated with friends and lovers throughout adolescence and adulthood. Thus, Carol-as-adult will find herself idealizing men on first encounter, only to be disillusioned each time they don't live up to her unrealistic image of a boyfriend. Similarly, she'll get into friendships with strong women on whom she'll get overly dependent, and then capsize the friendships by getting overly competitive with them. Then too, she'll worry that if she spends all her time with her boyfriends, her girlfriends will resent it. But if she backs off from the man to placate her girlfriends, she'll feel cheated and resentful and may even worry that they'll take him away.

Neurotics, then, are people whose childhood conflicts persist into adulthood as a set of ideas, images, and attitudes, and make trouble in relationships. Whereas unruly people are too uninhibited in their actions, neurotics are too inhibited. Inhibition, in fact, is the hallmark of neurosis. This is because so much of their mental life is stuck in childhood—they retain too vivid mental images of overpowering parental figures, and fear the pangs of conscience these images punish them with (Freud thought that the superego was based on these parental images). At the same time, they fear punishment and censure by other people whom they subconsciously identify with their mental images of their parents. These factors combine to make neurotics fearful and inhibited. Thus, when a therapist finds inhibition, a generalized fearfulness, and a preoccupation with triangular problems in relationships, he tends to diagnose a neurotic problem. The treatment offered is usually some form of talking therapy, which, if there's to be any hope of undoing the conflicts, will take a long time—usually a number of years.

I belabor these details to help us understand the group that mimics the neurotics. They probably represent a significant (if not the major) segment of what looks like especially severe cases of neurosis. They share the inhibitions and fearfulness of the neurotic, and sometimes even the preoccupation with Oedipal triangles—but their difficulties are rooted in one of the biologically treatable disorders. If they have neurotic conflicts (and anyone who's been a child does), these are made much worse by the psychiatric disorder. Because of all this, talking therapy goes even slower than with pure neurotics, if it goes at all. Unfortunately, when treatment bogs down, the therapist and patient often don't recognize that the patient has a biological disorder that's not responsive to talking therapy. Instead, they conclude that it's an unusually severe neurosis and hammer away at it—sometimes for decades. This can be a terrible waste of time for people whose psychiatric conditions have much simpler and very much less time-consuming treatments.

In my experience, the conditions most likely to be misdiagnosed as neurotic are mild mood disorders and mild or circumscribed phobias. The chronically discontent, procrastinating, and inhibited dysthymic, for example, can look like a neurotic paralyzed by his conflicts. The social phobic who's afraid of public speaking, or the agoraphobic who's fearful of traveling to new places, can look like neurotics immobilized by a conflict between exhibition and guilt. The rituals or preoccupations of a person with mild OCD can look like the irrationally fastidious attention to detail that characterizes many neurotics.

The case of John Dalton shows how all the textbook elements of neurosis can appear with a biologically based mood disorder, and therefore be completely resistant to both talking therapy and the passage of time.

The Pseudo-eternal Triangle: The Case of John Dalton

John Dalton wasn't the sort of person you'd think would spend years in a psychiatrist's office. When I met him, he was an engineering professor with a distinguished career at a prestigious university, hundreds of publications, dozens of patents, as well as devoted friends and admiring colleagues all over the world. He was gregarious, easygoing, and generous, whether of his extensive knowledge (both practical and academic) or of his time and money. If anyone's computer wouldn't work, he called John; if anyone needed a good biography of Copernicus or a six-letter word for economic upheaval, he called John. "Neurotic" wasn't a word people would apply to him.

Unless you were his girlfriend. In that case, you'd feel there was something very neurotic about him. Despite his boundless goodwill and generosity, at no time in his forty-five years had he been able to stay in a relationship. As soon as he'd find a girlfriend, he'd start up with a second one, and keep both going until one or the other found him out. Then one or both would leave in a huff, and the game would start again. Sometimes, however, neither woman would give up, and each would hang in there and compete for him. At times like this John was miserable. He knew how much he was distressing each woman, but he couldn't help it. He simply couldn't make a choice. This was what had brought him into treatment with me.

John had frustrated a generation of Freudians. How to account for a man being so well adjusted in so many areas and so outrageous in just one? The consensus was that John was deeply neurotic—enmeshed in prototypically Oedipal issues from a traumatic childhood. He had a hidden store of rage at women which was a response to his withholding mother, and a deep fear of men because of his overbearing father. Thus he hid away from men and tormented women with his indecision. That John didn't think of his mother as withholding or of his father as overbearing was seen as proof of severe repression and resistance to treatment. Thus they insisted on years of analysis.

It wasn't only John, however, who found his parents different from the analysts' image of them. Everyone who'd known them had found them just as unwithholding and unoverbearing as their son. But John's trouble with women hadn't budged over the years, and so he kept at therapy. In fairness, the analysts were doing their best—but nothing they did helped. In fairness too, their concept of neurosis is in general very useful. The problem is that it describes things that are so universal that they're easy to apply whether they fit all the facts or not.

Fortunately for John, there's another way to think about his problems. Indecision and procrastination are common symptoms of depression as well as of neurosis. A depressive's vulnerability to loss makes him afraid to lose whichever choice he doesn't make. To protect himself, therefore, he avoids decisions altogether. Since life involves a decision at every turn, this leads to a tendency to procrastinate—especially about decisions that involve losing connection with one or more people. The depressive's lack of energy and initiative, and his sense that nothing he tries will work, also contribute. Putting something off spares him the indignity of what he's sure will be another failure. Of course people procrastinate for any number of reasons—but when it's as enduring and resistant to treatment as it was for John, it usually indicates a depression or other major psychiatric disorder.

I wondered about this when the colleague who referred him first told me about John. Meeting him removed all doubt. When discussing his problems with women, he said that as far back as he could remember, he'd never been without a girlfriend. Why was that? Because he liked women and liked being around them. Could there be more to it—like not liking to be alone? He said he didn't know, it just never seemed to happen. I told him that I'd noticed that people who don't like to be alone, or are afraid to be alone, who can't make decisions and who procrastinate, are often depressed—even if they don't look that way or even feel that way. I didn't tell him that it's the same for people who constantly do things for others. Deep down they're needy for emotional support, and fulfill their needs by helping others. For one thing, they get a good deal of support in return. And subconsciously, by identifying with the people they support, they share the feeling with them.

Since John thought all this made sense, I started him on a trial of antidepressants. After a few weeks he found that not only could he endure being alone, but that he also liked being alone. He'd sit and read or go on walks, thinking his thoughts or dreaming his daydreams for the first time in his life without continuous companionship. He realized that up till then he had been afraid to be alone, and that he'd surrounded himself with women and students and friends and projects in order to avoid that situation. Thinking about this, he was by turns amused, embarrassed, and then saddened over the amount of time and energy he'd spent orchestrating such uninterrupted accompaniment.

At the same time, he felt an escalating discomfort with carrying on two relationships at once. It took some time to play out various fantasies of what life would be like with one or the other girlfriend. This generated a good deal of anxiety, medication notwithstanding. Nonetheless, in the matter of a few more weeks, he chose one.

Distinguishing someone who's very neurotic on a purely psychological basis from someone who's pseudo-neurotic on a biochemical basis is more difficult than it is for the earlier groups. The chronic low self-esteem of a dysthymic, the immobilization of a mild agoraphobic, the rituals and preoccupations of someone with mild OCD—all these look just like neurosis. I can offer a few helpful guidelines, but I can't make it easy.

As in John's case, the inability to be alone in someone who's not as impaired as a borderline personality suggests depression. The inability to make a decision also points to depression. Likewise, a stereotypic quality to rituals or preoccupations points to OCD—neurotic symptoms aren't usually quite so circumscribed (though they can be). When someone who isn't very unusual or very unruly is in psychotherapy for a very long time, you have to consider whether a biochemical disorder is complicating the case. There are two errors that must be avoided. The first is thinking that because a condition is mild, it's purely psychological. A mild disorder like dysthymia has just as biochemical a basis as a severe depression—and responds in the same way to medication. Likewise, a neurosis can be very severe but have its basis only in psychological experience. The second error is not understanding that two conditions can coexist. It's easy to convince yourself, for example, that John Dalton is neurotic—but that doesn't mean he's not also dysthymic. In reality, he's both. Anyone with a biochemical disorder started out with parents, after all, and was therefore susceptible to the three-sided conflicts that lead to neurosis.

CHAPTER 8

POPULAR MISCONCEPTIONS: WHY PEOPLE WON'T SWALLOW EVEN THE IDEA OF MEDICATION

The grass is always greener on the other side of the fence, and the brownest patch in the psychiatrist's yard, compared to that of the purely medical doctor, is how much work it takes to win the cooperation of his patients. "You have appendicitis, Mrs. Smith," says the surgeon to his patient with lower-right-quadrant pain, "and I'm going to take out the problem." The patient complies, the offending organ comes out, and Mrs. Smith is forever grateful. If, on the other hand, Mrs. Smith has obsessive-compulsive disorder (OCD), she may never even make it to a psychiatrist's office, and, if she does, she's likely to frustrate her doctor's therapeutic intentions by clinging to any of the dozen or so fallacies about medication I'll discuss in a moment. This hurts—knowing that a million Mrs. Smiths suffer in silence and solitude, and that a few milligrams a day of Prozac or Paxil could rescue them from their torment. It hurts too to know that for additional millions of people who are clinically depressed, the same few milligrams could save not only their livelihoods and relationships but, in fact, quite often their very lives.

How a psychiatrist feels about all this is softened by the fact that these are people he doesn't know. The situation is much more poignant and difficult for the partner or family member of someone whose life is being undone by a disorder he refuses to have treated. People consult me continually about partners or family members, only to find that despite my suggestion that treatment seems indicated, the person refuses. It's the same situation, I imagine, for someone who finds his partner in what he's read here but can't convince him to read the book, have an evaluation, or even to discuss the ideas. If you're stuck in this circumstance, I think this chapter will help you deal with the resistance you're meeting. I think it can also help a person who finds something of himself here, but is still debating whether he should seek help.

In general, resistances to appropriate treatment are consequences of the problems that need fixing in the first place: the disorder itself, how a person deals with it, and the resulting difficulties with relationships. The guilty depressive, for example, feels undeserving of help, so he doesn't seek it. The person with OCD worries that treatment will contaminate him, so he avoids it. The paranoid schizophrenic feels that the doctor wants to incriminate him, so he speaks in tongues, and so on. The following are a dozen popular misconceptions people use to squirm away from treatment—to the exasperation of partners, family, or friends who may know something about what psychiatry can do for them. I've divided these plausible-sounding but fundamentally unfounded resistances into four categories. I've found that organizing lists of psychological phenomena according to general themes like this is useful in stimulating further ideas and entries to the list.

Note first that there are some very good reasons to be reluctant to use medication or any other medical treatment. Doctors are fallible and drug companies are fallible, and as we all know, each group has done harm to a number of individuals because error, undue optimism, oversight, or naïveté let them prescribe or release medications that caused trouble. In Chapter Ten we will discuss detailed ways to scrutinize your doctor and his treatment methods in order to minimize any chance that they'll do you harm.

I should add that, if you're a depressive, antidepressant treatment, at least, will probably prolong your life. This is partly by keeping you out of the sixteen percent group who commit suicide, and partly because people who aren't depressed seem to live longer. You must weigh these observations against any speculation you may have about harmful long-term effects of the medication.

Resistance to Medication as Interpersonal Agenda

Whether it's winning the respect of a partner, keeping one's faith in authority, maintaining self-control, coping with the trauma of a bad childhood, or any other common psychological agenda, most of us are motivated by (and sometimes preoccupied with) one or more psychological agendas—especially when times are bad enough to drive us to a psychiatrist's office. The following four sections show how preoccupations with these agendas can keep people out of treatment or make trouble as soon as treatment gets under way.

"My husband/wife/partner won't respect me if I take medication."

The belief quoted here spells trouble whether it reflects the partner's actual attitude or not. Suppose it's not true; a wife incorrectly believes that her husband would react badly. This misperception is especially likely if she's depressed, because her low self-esteem makes it impossible for her to imagine anyone respecting her. Thus she thinks her husband will not respect her taking medication for her depression. The odds are she's wrong: Almost all spouses are delighted when their partner recovers from depression or any other serious condition—no matter what it took to make this happen.

On the other hand, if the spouse will in fact demean his partner for taking medication—"You're cranky today; go take your medicine"—this also spells trouble. Except in those (relatively rare) cases in which he is in fact abusive, his demeaning attitude is usually based on ignorance: He just doesn't know enough about emotional disorders to understand his partner's difficulties and what needs to be done about them. Usually an hour or two of a psychiatrist's time is enough to enlist his cooperation, by disabusing him of one or more of the misconceptions covered in this chapter.

Still, in a small number of cases, the spouse remains an obstacle to treatment despite the psychiatrist's explanations. Chances are that he's a person who, for his own emotional needs, requires a companion who's impaired. Perhaps he feels that she'll leave him if she recovers, or that after treatment he won't be able to control her, or that through treatment she'll become strong enough to control him. These couples need help. The good news is that when one partner responds to psychiatric treatment, couples therapy is usually remarkably effective in resolving the other partner's misguided attitudes.

Thus, whether a person's fears are groundless (as they normally are) or justified (as they occasionally are), perseverance usually pays off. I can recall only one case in which a good response to psychiatric treatment hastened the end of a relationship.

"You can't trust doctors anymore."

As the old saw goes, just because you're paranoid doesn't mean they're not out to get you. Likewise, just because you don't trust your doctor doesn't mean you're paranoid. In fact, if you don't question your doctor, you're probably not paranoid enough. A patient must be his own advocate, and this includes getting his questions answered. Questioning the doctor is especially important these days under "managed care," when specialists are assigned by insurance companies' profit-based guidelines rather than by open referrals by generalists to the particular specialists they think are the most competent. Chapter Ten will offer some practical guidelines for evaluating doctors and insurance companies.

As in most things, coming to trust a psychiatrist merits a balanced approach. Only a fool does everything he's told, even by an alleged expert; still, there comes a point when a patient needs to accept that the doctor is on his side and, after years of training and practice, is likely to know something about treating patients. In my experience, anyone who can't negotiate this balance usually has trouble trusting people generally, especially in close relationships. Trust is a very delicate matter, built up throughout childhood, and consolidated—or eroded—over the course of adolescence and adulthood. It's an especially difficult issue for people susceptible to psychiatric disorders. A depressive, for example, has difficulty trusting because he's so easily hurt emotionally. The attention disordered person has trouble trusting because his difficulty understanding the world makes him feel continually ambushed, and therefore continually betrayed.

It's a lot to ask a person who finds it impossible to trust a doctor to get some perspective on his difficulties with trust, and then to get past them. Anyone vulnerable enough to consider psychiatric help doesn't drop his guard very easily. But I'll ask him anyway—at least to try. To whatever extent you're able to ask yourself if your distrust of psychiatry is an aspect of a more general problem with trust, the more likely you are to gain some perspective on the situation—and then to let someone help you.

On the other hand, if you're the partner of someone who you'd like to have see a psychiatrist but his difficulty with trust is an obstacle, you'll have to ask yourself the same question about him. You may sense, however, that it would be inflammatory to raise this concern with him—especially if he has trouble trusting you—and you're probably right. If in doubt, don't do it. It's probably more useful to implement your concern with action. You can, for example, agree with him that any doctor needs to be assessed carefully, and that two heads are better than one— and then go with him to an appointment. One tactic I've seen work for people trying to nurture a capacity to trust in a partner is to suggest going to a couples therapy group (or to therapy just for the two of you if this seems more palatable). Or your partner may be more willing to join a therapy group without you. In either case, group therapy is a good way to help a person begin to develop trust. For one thing, the fact that several people are present makes the interactions less intense, and thus less threatening, than the one-on-one relationships in individual therapy. Also, a person can hang out on the shore, so to speak, until he's ready to test, and then begin to trust, the waters. Then too, there's a sense of security that people feel in groups—a safety in numbers—that makes them a useful environment for developing trust. In a sense, it's a second chance for a person to grow up in the nurturant family setting that so many of us have never known.

"Doesn't taking medication mean I'm losing control?"

This worry is related to the preceding one, but involves a different aspect of the capacity to trust. Everyone is sensitive to issues of control in relationships, but for some the issues are especially troubling. People with obsessive-compulsive personalities, for example, have an especially hard time with these issues; they demand excessive control in their relationships because they fear that everyone else is trying to control them. Let me remind you what I said in Chapter Four: The obsessive-compulsive personality—the obsessional, for short—and obsessive-compulsive disorder (OCD) are different. They are related only in the similarity of their symptoms, a fact that for decades misled psychiatry into thinking that OCD was an exaggerated form of the obsessive-compulsive personality and would therefore respond to the same purely psychological treatment. The obsessive-compulsive personality is a personality style that pervades everything a person does or thinks. OCD, on the other hand, is a circumscribed set of obsessions or compulsions beyond which the personality may be more or less normal.

There's something of the obsessional in all of us—thus what I'm going to say here will apply to some extent to most people. It's the part that gets us into control struggles and that fears losing control in an unfamiliar adventure like seeing a psychiatrist. Recognizing an aspect of it in yourself or in your partner can help you get the fears and struggles out of the way. Fortunately, this personality type isn't hard to recognize—even in yourself. Beyond the need for control, the obsessional personality is marked by orderliness, stubbornness, stinginess, and a maddening degree of attention to detail. Obsessionals also tend to be constricted in the expression of emotion, and present a sort of gray exterior to the world. Their thinking, however, has no gray whatsoever; it's strictly black-or-white, all-or-nothing.

The slightest lapse strikes the obsessional as a complete loss of control. An obsessional may fear, for example, that he's losing his mind if a crisis brings him a single sleepless night, or that he's being shamefully unfaithful if attracted, however superficially, to anyone but his partner. Thus it's no surprise that the emergence of a disorder like depression or agoraphobia or even OCD strikes him as an unthinkable loss of control. When a partner raises the question of such a disorder, or a psychiatrist diagnoses it, he feels out of control and, in his all-or-nothing way, deals with the circumstances by denying it altogether. In measured speech and emotionless tones he explains that no, your logic is flawed, that there's a purely logical explanation for his depressive immobility, or obsessions, or phobias, and that in fact he's a paragon of sanity and control—perhaps even more than he'd realized before you so carelessly raised the question of his stability, and gave him the opportunity to think more carefully about it. All the while he makes you feel like a simple-minded, fuzzy-thinking flake who's trying to seduce him into an orgy of the irrationality and unpredictability of all things psychological. The same debate goes on internally if you have a degree of obsessionality yourself, and try to get past your control issues and into treatment.

Nonetheless, you do need to raise the question of a psychiatric disorder if you suspect one—either in yourself or in your partner. And if you find that either of you is concerned that seeking treatment may mean losing control, you need to ask yourself whether this is a part of how you or he deal with life generally—that is, by controlling it. It's far too much to ask anyone to guide himself or his partner past the tendency toward overcontrollingness—but whatever perspective you can get on the matter will make it easier to allow yourself or your partner to get appropriate help. The doctor can then help you deal with the control issues, and the treatment itself can help reduce the overemphasis on control. That is, besides the benefit of helping the primary disorder, a good result from treatment represents a reward for coming to treatment. This, along with the greater sense of security and competence that follows recovery from a psychiatric disorder, makes a good start toward reducing the need for rigid control of everything. In addition, psychotherapy aimed at the overcontrolling behavior tends to work more efficiently with this double boost from psychiatric treatment.

"Medication won't change my miserable childhood."

The literal truth of this statement makes it compelling and formidable as a roadblock to treatment. Psychologically, however, the statement is not true. That is, how a person feels about his childhood depends on how he feels as he recalls it. Someone in a wonderful mood, such as just after falling in love, thinks of everything past, present, and future as wonderful. People who are depressed sometimes remember their childhood as wonderful, and spend the present mourning its passing; more commonly, they recall childhood as miserable along with everything else in their lives. Psychologically, then, the past is subject to change, depending on a person's mood.

The past is also subject to change depending on a person's psychological agendas. As we've seen over and over, most people put a great deal of psychological effort into being able to feel good about themselves. Many people do this by making victimhood their way of life, by wearing a miserable or abusive past like a badge of honor. They exaggerate its misery in their recollection, or dwell on its actual miseries excessively—and feel that this makes them admirable for having endured such a childhood. Quite often the formerly abused child wreaks a belated and displaced revenge on his present-day partner by provoking the partner into abusing him—thereby making the partner appear morally reprehensible and himself morally superior for enduring him. The processes are all subliminal, making them all the more powerful because they're not subject to conscious scrutiny. The combined sense of superiority and revenge provides a powerful gratification that is difficult to give up. We can say, then, that they refuse treatment because their misery is too compelling.

It's difficult enough for a therapist with training and experience to break through this defensive armor—I wouldn't recommend trying to impose it on someone you love (even if you yourself are a therapist). But I do think that keeping the ideas in mind can help you keep out of the trap of gratifying a partner's wishes for gaining sympathy and admiration at the price of provoking abuse. Not taking the bait and not being provoked into abusing people like this is probably the best way get them into treatment.

If, on the other hand, you think that psychiatry can help with your personal or relationship difficulties but you hear the tones of this mantra of misery echoing through your mind, try your best to understand that its gratifications are counterfeit. Life has far greater gratifications than misery, and there's an army of therapists of various stripes devoted to helping you find them.

Resistance to Medication As Symptom of a Psychiatric Disorder

As I said earlier, in many cases resistance to treatment is the direct result of a person's symptoms. This is hardly surprising; a person relates to a doctor and his tools in the same way he relates to people and things in general, and we've seen all along how badly psychiatric disorders can disrupt these relations.

The following two questions are examples of psychiatric symptoms as resistance to treatment that are common and troublesome, especially since their basis in symptomatology isn't always so clear.

"What will become of me if *this* fails too?"

Hopelessness is central to the experience of depression. All the world is bleak, and the future holds no possibility of change for the better. When a depressive is told that his suffering is biologically determined and can be treated with medication, his reaction is the same as it is to any optimistic message: He doesn't believe it. It takes at least a glimmer of hope for a person to let himself go to a psychiatrist's office. Working against this hope is the fear that this is his last chance, and he's terribly afraid that this final opportunity will fail once he risks pursuing it.

Thus, to avoid that final—and to his mind, inevitable—disappointment, he resists going for help, and even when he does decide to go, he procrastinates endlessly about making an appointment. A partner can help a person trapped in this dilemma to see that his reluctance and fear are symptoms of his depression. Further, he can explain that there are a large number of treatments available—a wide range of antidepressant medication, countless combinations and augmentations of these, and some newer and promising new techniques on the horizon. As treatment begins, he must be assured that this is not his last chance: All is not lost if the first few attempts to use medication fail (as they do in some ten or twenty percent of cases that eventually succeed). It will be difficult for him to believe this (or for you, if you're the one who's depressed), but it's true nonetheless—hopelessness and pessimism are depressive symptoms, not psychiatric realities.

"There's nothing wrong with my brain, so I don't need anyone to fix it."

No one likes to be told that something is wrong with his brain. It's a terrible injury to one's sense of oneself and to one's pride to be told that this most vital of organs is defective. Nonetheless, the reason people resist the idea of a defect in their brain chemistry so strongly goes beyond pride: It's because deep down they know it's true. In my experience, people with psychiatric disorders almost always know something's wrong with how their minds work. This awareness is most palpable for people with ADD. All their lives they've known that something is amiss. As children they saw classmates sit still, be calm, and learn, and wondered what it was that kept them from doing the same. All through school and later at work they felt inferior to those who did better or were promoted faster or who simply learned or worked or got ahead much more easily. At the same time, they were constantly criticized: In school they were called lazy or stupid, at work they were called careless or inefficient, and in relationships they were called inattentive or inadequate. Theirs is the constant experience of insult added to injury.

Similar feelings are found in all people with significant mental disorders. Schizophrenics know that most people can think more clearly than they do, and that others are not tormented by hallucinations and delusions. People with OCD are especially prone to feel hopelessly flawed by their obsessions and compulsions, and to feel that only they suffer with these symptoms. Depressives, too, know that other people aren't oppressed by interminable periods of black mood and inability to function. In each case, the toll on self-esteem is tremendous. Healthy self-esteem is supported by a sense of being in control of oneself and being able to function adequately; when a person realizes, subliminally or overtly, that he's not in control of himself or of his capacities, his self-esteem plummets. People can rarely endure such injury to their pride, and many of them deal with this by denying that it's true. When someone points out what they've really known all along, they can't afford to set aside their denial to collude with such a villain.

There are several ways to help a partner (or yourself) past this impasse. One is to compare a psychiatric disorder to other biochemical disorders and to ask why a problem with brain chemistry should be any more reprehensible than a problem with any other organ such as those leading to diabetes or hemophilia. Another is to adopt a global perspective and point out that given the lunacy and improprieties of our species (from criminality and war to talk show hosts and congressmen), something has to be wrong with a large proportion of all our brains. These perspectives help a person feel less uniquely and personally flawed—because his brain shares its chemical deficiencies with a number of other organs, and he shares his personal deficiencies with a great many other people.

Resistance to Medication As an Institutional Icon

A person's relationship to the institutions in his life, whether his marriage, his country club, or his country, help form his attitudes toward his emotional problems. Unfortunately, people with significant psychopathology relate to institutions in the same problematic way they do to individuals. Paranoids, for example, routinely suspect that the FBI or CIA is after them (it's never the IRS—why is that?). Hostile depressives demand an unreasonable degree of nurturance from their family, community, or place of employment, and begrudge them for not complying with their typically impossible demands. As the following two examples show, allegiance even to upstanding organizations like Alcoholics Anonymous or the institution of psychoanalysis can reach symptomatic proportions, and keep many people from getting the treatment they need. In each section I'll counter two high-sounding but troublesome statements associated with these groups.

"I don't want any mind-altering substances in my system."

Alcoholics Anonymous and its many spinoff groups have been sensationally useful to millions of people. Nonetheless, one idea held by many AA members causes a good deal of trouble. It is by no means an official position of the organization itself, but it's entrenched enough to have done a disservice to many members—sometimes a terminal disservice. The idea is that any mind-altering substance, be it alcohol, a street drug, or a psychiatric drug, must be avoided. Some members are quite strident on the point, as people often are when they don't understand what they're talking about. Unfortunately, in group settings stridency tends to shout down reason, and many members absorb the idea without thinking it through or studying the facts involved. In the process, many members with treatable psychiatric disorders are cheated out of the opportunity for treatment.

If I hadn't seen this attitude precipitate suicides and other disasters for AA members, I'd find the following prototypic incarnation of its message amusing. It's by no means rare for a patient to tell me that for decades he's abused alcohol, cocaine, amphetamines, marijuana, PCP, and tobacco, and that he's lost countless jobs, several wives, custody of all his children, and his health to these drugs. But when I suggest an antidepressant for the depression underlying much of this madness, he assumes a posture of disdain, and with a straight face tells me that using mind-altering chemicals like those is reprehensible. Someone like him never sees the humor of his convictions, and to point it out would only antagonize him. What does work, sometimes, is a persistent, objective explanation of the facts involved.

What he needs to learn is that contrary to his intuition, his drugs and the psychiatrist's drugs are exactly opposite in their effect. Alcohol, cocaine, and the like alter the mind by pushing brain activity away from normal. Anyone who walks into a party full of strangers, for example, feels anxiety; it's a perfectly normal response. If he drinks alcohol to calm the anxiety, he's moving his brain into a state that although it's more comfortable, isn't natural; calmness when entering a roomful of strangers simply isn't part of our genetic endowment. If he keeps drinking because he likes the comfort and confidence it gives him, then he's pushing his brain more and more out of equilibrium—an act for which it wreaks its revenge the next morning. On the other hand, when a patient takes antidepressant or mood-stabilizing medication, he's pushing his brain back toward normal functioning. Put simply, street drugs give you the rush of your brain working abnormally, while medication gives you the relief of having it back working normally. When a person is on an appropriate dose of an antidepressant, he doesn't feel anything unusual—not sedation, not euphoria. The only change he feels is that his psychiatric symptoms are gone.

Another common concern is that psychiatric medications are addictive. This worry almost always comes from unfamiliarity with the medications. Only one group of psychiatric medications can become addicting, and then only if used inappropriately. These are the minor tranquilizers (chemically speaking, the benzodiazepines); if used at too high doses for too long, they can be addicting. Xanax, Halcion, and Ativan are most likely to become addicting because of their short duration of action. (The shorter the duration of action of a drug, the more addicting; this is why crack cocaine, for example, is so addicting.) Fortunately, even if someone does become addicted to one of the benzodiazepines, it's usually a simple matter to taper him off it. For the shorter-acting medications, it may be necessary first to switch to a longer-acting member of the class, and then to taper that medication down over a period of days or weeks.

On the other hand, the antidepressants, antipsychotics, mood stabilizers, and other of the psychiatrist's medications are not addictive. It is true that if any of these is stopped abruptly, there may be a so-called rebound reaction, with a return of the original symptoms, sometimes along with nausea, confusion, dizziness, or other relatively mild symptoms. The reaction almost never occurs, though, if the medications are tapered appropriately. Again, medications with a short duration of action give the worst rebound reactions. The biggest danger comes with abruptly stopping the antidepressants; this can lead to an abrupt onset of severe depression. This isn't an example of addiction, however; it's a case of using the medication incorrectly.

"Medication just masks the underlying problems."

A significant segment of the psychoanalytic community promotes the concern that medication *masks* emotional problems, and thereby robs people of the opportunity to solve them. The argument given is that using medication to treat depression or obsessions or compulsions is a mere quick fix compared to the ideal solution (the gold standard, analysts like to say): spending years on the couch analyzing the psychological roots of the problem. My psychiatric and psychoanalytic training were at a time when this argument went unquestioned among a great many psychoanalytically oriented psychiatrists as well as among many, if not most, psychologists, social workers, and other nonmedical psychotherapists. It was clear even then that the statement was based more on prejudice and preference than on clinical experience, and was most popular with therapists who couldn't or wouldn't prescribe medication.

In most circumstances, clinical experience (reality's gold standard, after all) demonstrates quite the opposite of the above dictum. People who are depressed or psychotic, for example, show more, not less, ability and willingness to tackle their problems when they're adequately medicated, and therefore do much better in therapy. There are a number of reasons for this. Some are practical: The depressed patient now has more energy to devote to treatment, the attention disordered patient has greater ability to focus on treatment, the psychotic patient is less distracted by his hallucinations and delusions, the manic patient can sit still long enough to complete a sentence.

Medication also restores the patient's use of logic and abstraction. In severe cases of psychiatric impairment, the higher, more abstract levels of thought are the most impaired. A patient I saw during a psychotic episode, for example, complained that his mother had poisoned him. As a moderate dose of antipsychotic medication and daily therapy sessions helped him recover, he began to think in progressively more abstract terms. Instead of thinking that his mother had poisoned his food, he began to complain that she was making him feel bad by enacting some (unspecified) magical rituals. As recovery proceeded, he said that his mother had always made him feel bad because of the way she talked to him. At this point, several weeks into treatment, he had finally come to understand that his delusion of being poisoned was a concrete expression (the best he could do while psychotic) of the idea that by continually telling him that people are no good and likely to hurt him, she undermined his ability to trust them, thereby impairing his ability to make friends. Thus, rather than covering up the issues, medication made them much more available for understanding and resolution.

It is true, on the other hand, that in some cases medication can obstruct a patient's ability to utilize psychotherapy, namely when various minor tranquilizers are prescribed to manage mild degrees of anxiety—usually by nonpsychiatric physicians—when talking therapy would be more appropriate. Treatment with these medications is appropriate only when the patient's anxiety seriously disrupts his mental functioning, as in panic attacks, severe phobias, or severe cases of generalized anxiety disorder. Even in those cases it's usually best to use a minor tranquilizer only at the start of treatment (because they work so quickly) and a slower-acting antidepressant or antipsychotic to control the symptoms over time. Antidepressants and antipsychotics don't work by masking anxiety; they treat the panic or agitation associated with a psychiatric disorder by returning a person's mental functioning to normal. In cases of mild anxiety the analysts are right; mild anxiety can be a useful tool to indicate areas of psychological conflict, and as motivation to resolve them (so that the unpleasant anxiety will go away).

Resistance to Medication As Psychological Style (One's Relationship to One's Own Mind)

The human psyche being what it is (an anarchy of sub-selves struggling for expression and dominance), dealing with oneself involves a set of relationships that parallel a person's relationships with other people. One of Freud's greatest insights was that in psychiatric disorders the components of the psyche conflict with one another, while in mental health the mind can accommodate and orchestrate these parts simultaneously. When the question of medication comes up, for example, the systems of a person's mind all begin shouting demands. Most vocal here are the subsystems of pride, identity, imagery (of self and others), and that omnipresent built-in bully, conscience. The following sections deal with the outbursts of opinion erupting from these systems the moment the idea of medication comes up.

Pride: "The very idea of medication devalues the human spirit."

I quote this from a manicky English teacher whose philanderings and investment schemes had so annihilated his family's fortunes and so taxed his wife's and children's goodwill that his pride (spirit, he called it) was all he had left to rely on. This, of course, is what pride is for: to shore up one's sense of self when it's about to crumble. The reason, then, that pride plays so central a role in human life is that assaults on one's sense of self are so continual and dangerous. These start with the earliest indignities like being literally unable to hold your head up, and persist through a lifespan of times when you can barely hold up your head, figuratively, in the face of disapproving parents, teachers, clergymen, or supervisors—all accompanied by the inner scoldings of conscience and the echoes of past humiliations. For many people the ultimate blow to pride is that the spirit is not in charge even of itself, and that the workings of strange chemicals in the brain and in the psychiatrist's pillbox are going to take charge of their very mind, brain, and spirit. In the face of this blow, pride often turns to the simplest, and maddest, defense: It denies the issue entirely and shouts, no, you're wrong, I am in charge here.

The mind, then, is loath to admit its impotence in the face of its chemical derangements, and pride is its way of denying the need for help. Thus, holding up the human spirit as something morally greater and ethically finer than a scientific understanding of brain mechanisms is a way for pride to assert (and comfort) itself. This conviction—that attention to the biochemistry of mental processes demeans the human spirit—displays a degree of all-or-nothing logic that would make the staunchest obsessional blush with envy. There is no reason for a biochemical understanding of a person's anguish to preclude a psychological or spiritual understanding of it. No sensible psychiatrist needs to ignore the psychological or spiritual aspects of his patient's experience because he tries to normalize his biochemistry—and vice versa.

The Sense of Reality: "If I take medication, I won't know what's real."

It isn't the medication but the psychiatric disorder that can confound the ability to assess reality. During my psychiatric training I treated a twenty-four-year-old man who had smoked marijuana every day for the last twelve years. He didn't tell me this though—an omission that led to months and months of treatment with no progress whatever. Marijuana can intensify mood swings in someone with a mood disorder. For this man it produced a set of absolutely regular and completely uncontrollable swings of mood. Every two weeks he experienced a complete change of mental state. For two weeks he would be manicky: excessively optimistic, outgoing, expansive, and charming. The world was his oyster, no one or no thing could resist him, be it a pretty woman or a complex theme in philosophy, his hobby. The next two weeks, however, he would be depressed: gloomy, withdrawn, prickly, pessimistic, and suicidal. The world was then nonnegotiable, no one or no thing was accessible to him, not women, not philosophy, nothing whatever of what had all but fallen at his feet the two weeks before. Concealing his marijuana use, then, gave me an unusually clear view of the way mood affects how a person sees the world.

The ups and downs made me dizzy, but it caused him no confusion whatever. Every other two weeks he would say that the weeks before he'd been unreasonably optimistic (or pessimistic), that he'd understated (or overstated) the malice or impossibility of his world, and that I shouldn't have taken him so seriously back then; it was as if he lived in two different worlds (one a heaven, the other a hell), neither of which would acknowledge the other. This went on week after week—until he slipped up one day and told me about the marijuana, causing me to change his treatment.

The point is, reality shifts with mood: If you're depressed, the world seems bleak and unforthcoming; if you're manic, the world seems colorful and generous; and if your mood is normal, the world is a plausible mix of all these states of mind. I'm sure this observation has philosophical ramifications that would twist my mind into a pretzel (how many twists depending, I suppose, on my mood)—but practically, it's simply a fact of human nature.

Since all of us have an intuitive feeling for the variability of the sense of reality with mood, we all feel vulnerable to losing our objective grasp on it—especially with the extremes of mood present with psychiatric disorders. Thus people worry that if medication changes their mood, their reality sense will be further confused to the point that they won't know whether what they will experience is real. Fortunately, this worry is unrealistic. What almost always happens is that as a person recovers from a psychiatric disorder, he worries less about what's real and what isn't. His sense of reality is more intact; in the case of a mood disorder, for example, he's no longer so critical of everything about himself, including his ability to assess reality. I find that presenting these observations to people considering medication is comforting, and often helps them to accept the treatment they need.

Identity: "But who will I become if medication cures me?"

The sense of self is as thorny a concept as is the sense of reality. The challenge of defining the self, especially in the face of the chemical processes that can disrupt it, is an intoxicating intellectual enterprise—but watching someone suffer the effects of these processes quickly brings us back to the sober realities of the matter.

To a mentally healthy person, questions of self and identity may be intriguing, but they're not matters of urgency. To someone in the throes of a serious mental breakdown, on the other hand, they become matters of psychological life or death—something difficult to comprehend for someone who's never had the experience. This suggests that the person's anguish about losing his sense of self is itself a symptom of his disorder. In fact, as patients recover, the pain and preoccupation with problems of self and identity diminish along with the other symptoms. The underlying questions may remain, but not the degree of anguish about them. Especially with depressives, I find that the level of concern about identity is a useful yardstick for gauging recovery. For people with less severe disorders, anxiety about identity is more muted, but nonetheless it's a common reason for hesitancy about psychiatric treatment.

I find that it's comforting for people struggling with issues of identity to suggest that who a person is is determined moment by moment by biochemically based processes, the underpinnings of which are coded in the DNA. Treatment returns a person to who he is (and who he feels he is) when his brain is in a normal biochemical state. Who you are, then, is yourself without the biochemical distortions of a psychiatric disorder; if it takes medication to restore this self, so be it. You will feel and know that this is the self you are. It's only when the self is not in its normal state that the question is so distressing.

The Conscience: "I should be able to do it myself."

The problem here is that the conscience (technically speaking, the superego) knows that the psyche's functioning is below par whenever it's afflicted by a psychiatric disorder. Since it's the business of the conscience to complain about inadequacies of any sort, it now complains all the louder. An intrinsic part of depression is that the conscience becomes much more imposing and holds the person to exceedingly high standards in all areas of experience including the emotional. We hear it fussing at the rest of the psyche to shape up and deal with matters at hand, without outside help. Unfortunately, if a person's resistance to treatment persists, a vicious circle is set up: The worse the depression becomes (as it can without treatment), the harsher the conscience becomes, thereby deepening the depression; this in turn strengthens the conscience, and on and on around the circle. In this way the escalating pressure can reach annihilatory proportions—a major factor in pushing a depressed person toward suicide.

Sometimes an exaggerated insistence on self-reliance is based on the belief that a mental disorder is one's own fault. Unfortunately, some people (including therapists with more imagination than training) like to insist that someone who's depressed is choosing to be that way. This is lunacy: No one chooses to be depressed, psychotic, or otherwise impaired, and to suggest this only makes a person feel guilty and hopeless. A person isn't responsible for how he feels, or for whether he's depressed; it's not a choice—feelings and moods come unbidden, and it adds insult (not insight) to injury to blame him for it. Telling this to people who feel that it's an indignity to accept help for a psychiatric disorder can help them forgive themselves for their disorder. It can also help to point out that people rarely do anything significant alone. We're a species that flourishes only by cooperation. We learn to walk and talk and read and write only with help—and there's no reason that it should be any different with learning to recover from a serious mental disorder.

All told, then, we've covered a dozen misconceptions about psychiatric medication. In the next chapters we turn to the practical details of getting help for the disorders we've discussed, and of making the best use of it.

CHAPTER 9

WHAT'S A COUPLE TO DO?

In this and the following chapter I'll offer some practical advice—first about how to find the right professional help, and then about how to make the best use of it. This chapter deals with finding the help—including details about what treatments are available and how to choose between types of treatment and between individuals practicing any one type.

Finding help for a relationship suffering from a psychiatric disorder is especially tough because it involves solving two problems simultaneously. One is understanding how his mental disorder affects one of the partners and how to treat him for it. The other is understanding how his disorder affects the relationship, and what to do about it. Getting help for this conceptual folie à deux means you'll need someone who can ride two horses at once, so to speak, or two people who get along well enough to ride two horses side by side—in either case over some very rocky terrain.

This is a big task, especially these days. For one thing, it's the age of specialization—there are more and more types of therapists to learn about and choose from. At the same time, the influence of managed care is putting a good deal of this specialty care out of reach of many people. And it seems likely that all fields, including mental health, will become more specialized with time. Specializing appeals to therapists. It's easier, for example, to stay at one pole of the psychology-biology spectrum rather than at a more realistic position somewhere in the middle. It's easy to envy the old-time psychoanalysts, for example, who could sit hour after hour, year after year, focusing on purely psychological issues—without concern for cost effectiveness, peer review, insurance forms, medically treatable disorders, or any other of a million present-day headaches. Likewise, the consulting psychopharmacologist (a specialist in psychiatric medication) has an enviable job: See a patient, make a diagnosis, prognosis, and recommendations—then leave to others the chore of implementing your ideas, working through a patient's resistance to treatment, getting authorization from the managed care company, dealing with the family, and on and on.

Recent trends in specialization have split the mental health field into a group that does counseling and psychotherapy (psychologists, social workers, counselors) and another that does medication and other biologically based treatments (psychiatrist). Many psychiatrists, of course, still do a good deal of psychotherapy, but fewer each decade. Within the group of psychotherapists are specialists in couples counseling, custody evaluation, family counseling, psychological testing, and so on. Likewise, many psychiatrists develop special expertise in one subset of mental disorders like schizophrenia and other psychotic disorders, mood disorders, attention disorders, and so on. As we saw in the Introduction, all this specializing can breed isolation, competition, and mutual devaluation. This in turn makes it all the more difficult to find a therapist who can handle the complexity of a relationship troubled by a psychiatric illness.

Before tackling this and other details of searching out and evaluating therapists, I'll say something about the most common types of therapists—how they differ in training, treatment philosophy, techniques, and so on.

The Varieties of Therapists

Mark Twain was fond of lampooning the 3,000 or so varieties of religion he'd found on the market—each with the one uniquely correct perspective on God and man. I'm sure he'd feel the same about the universe of therapists on the market these days. Fortunately, most therapists fall into a handful of groups. Here I'll narrow it to three.

(1) Psychiatrists

A psychiatrist is first trained as a medical doctor. He's been through medical school and internship, and then another three years of specialty training (called residency) in treating mental disorders. Residency programs differ, but they all teach a range of treatment modalities from talking therapy to various types of medically based treatment, especially the use of medication. However, in the past few decades the emphasis in training has shifted toward the biological—to the point that many patients (and older psychiatrists) complain that psychiatrists specialize too much in the direction of medical treatment and give short shrift to psychological treatment.

Psychiatrists working with seriously disturbed patients have the option of hospitalizing them. This is often necessary for patients who are violent, suicidal, or too impaired to care for themselves. Once in the hospital, a patient can be treated with medication, individual therapy, group therapy, family (or couples) therapy, educational programs, and other modalities best done on hospital wards. If you or your partner suffers from serious psychiatric problems, it's a good idea to work with one of those psychiatrists who has hospital privileges. This may limit your options, but having ready access to inpatient psychiatric care can be a matter of life or death.

Until the last few decades, psychoanalysts (analysts for short) were usually psychiatrists who, after completing residency, did a further six to ten years' training at a psychoanalytic institute. In recent years, many nonpsychiatrists, especially psychologists and social workers, have become psychoanalysts—though the United States has generally been behind other countries in this development. Another relatively new trend is that a number of patients are being psychoanalyzed while on medication—something that during my training was so blasphemous that its mere mention (let alone enactment) was as likely as not to provoke almost immediate expulsion from the fold.

A word here about nonpsychiatric physicians prescribing psychiatric medications. Any medical doctor has the right to prescribe these medications, and a great many do. Some do it well, but in my experience this isn't very common.

How the brain responds to medication is complex, and made even more so by the interaction of the brain and liver. Like the brain, the liver has a sophisticated capacity to handle foreign substances. Among its many functions, it rids the body of these by transforming them into chemical forms easier to excrete (by making them water soluble).

The subtleties of how the brain and liver handle foreign substances cause endless headaches for psychiatrists. Suppose, for example, you start a patient on an antidepressant and he does well. No sooner do you congratulate yourself on a good result than he's depressed again because his liver has learned to inactivate the medication more efficiently, and his brain has adjusted and stopped feeling its effect. So you raise the dose and wait to see if it happens again. In the meantime, the processes that are now clearing out the antidepressant more efficiently are also starting to clear out other (including nonpsychiatric) medications more efficiently. So now they need adjusting. Sometimes it goes the other way—the liver gets so busy with some hard-to-process medication that it has less capacity to process other medications. Now their levels rise because they're being processed and excreted more slowly. Prozac is probably the most notorious for this, and has the capacity to raise blood levels of other medications to as much as four times their pre-Prozac levels. To make this all the more difficult, the details of brain and liver chemistry vary tremendously from person to person. This means that any two people will need very different doses to maintain therapeutic brain and blood levels.

These and other complications can drive the calmest and most competent of psychiatrists to distraction—and they deal with this sort of thing every day, and don't need to deal with all the other organ systems and medical conditions that generalists have to content with. It's hard, therefore, for a generalist to have the necessary experience, time, or patience to fiddle with dosages and combinations of dosages for prescribing psychiatric medication. The moral here isn't never to let an internist or gynecologist treat your depression medically, but, rather, that you need to be sure that yours knows about what I'm discussing here. Tell him you've heard that unlike most medications in general medicine, doses of psychiatric medication vary tremendously between individuals, don't correlate with the severity of the disorder, and frequently need to be changed over time. If he scoffs, disagrees, or in other ways denies the significance of what you're telling him, get someone else to treat you psychiatrically.

Clinical Psychologists

Clinical psychologists are therapists who have a doctoral degree in psychology. Their training involves a number of years of course work, supervised clinical training, the completion of a research project relevant to clinical practice, and a period of clinical work before completing a comprehensive examination for licensing. Psychologists don't get medical training and therefore don't prescribe medication or have hospital admitting privileges.

Psychologists are trained to do talking therapy, but in so many different ways that it can be confusing to someone trying to choose one. The differences between different types of therapists can be quite profound: Freudian or Jungian therapists identify and help modify psychological issues left over from childhood; cognitive therapists identify and restructure their patients' belief systems; behavioral therapists reprogram patients' behavior, fears, and attitudes; Rogerian therapists reflect back patients' feelings; and so on through about 250 different schools.

One difference between psychiatrists and psychologists is that psychologists are trained in formal psychological testing: Rorschach tests, intelligence tests, and the like. These are designed to generate comprehensive diagnostic impressions, measurements of the components of intelligence, identification of specific psychological problems, appropriate topics for therapy, recommendations for effective therapy approaches, and other factors that may be difficult to identify or evaluate by interview alone. In cases with unresolved questions about diagnosis, psychological issues, appropriate treatment, and so on, a psychologist skilled in psychological testing can be very helpful.

Psychiatric Social Workers and Counselors

These are similar to psychologists. Like psychologists, they specialize in talking therapy, but usually have master's degrees, not doctorates. This means that they haven't written a doctoral level dissertation, but they've usually completed about as much course work and clinical training as psychologists—the requirements differ from state to state. I'm not sure the differences between the three groups are as important as the difference between individuals within any of the groups.

In recent years these groups are being used more frequently because they're more cost effective compared to the other groups; and in my experience, a good counselor or social worker is just as (or even more) competent as his psychiatric or psychologist colleagues. This is especially the case as opposed to a psychiatrist who's had the majority of his training in psychopharmacology at the expense of psychotherapy—a trend in many training centers these days.

However, a counselor without the medical training of a psychiatrist may well miss a psychiatric (or, worse, a purely medical) disorder. Here you'll have to be your own advocate, probably more than in any other situation we've encountered. If, after having read the first few chapters of this book, you suspect something beyond purely psychological factors is afoot (and your counselor doesn't), you'll need to act, and act effectively. The squeaky wheel gets the grease, remember, so you'll have to be vocal—a task that may be much easier for your partner than for you if you're the one impaired by what you fear may be a psychiatric disorder. Put your concerns and requests for second opinions in writing. This mobilizes therapists and insurance company administrators, pushing, I suspect, the magic button called: "potential lawsuit."

Choosing a Therapist for the Two of You

The question, are we dealing with an individual psychiatric or psychological problem (a depression, neurosis, and so on), or a couples problem (lack of communication skills, poor partner choice, or both), is as difficult as it is important. Everything I've written to this point has been to help you begin to answer it. If one of you is suffering from what's clearly a psychiatric disorder and the relationship doesn't seem to be overly disrupted by it—then only the affected partner may need treatment. The other partner is then available for support, information, and so on. In the (probably more common) situation in which there's an identifiable disorder and it's causing distress between partners, then you'll need to find a therapist (or therapists) who can handle both the disorder and its effects.

If you're not sure whether there is a psychiatric disorder in one (or both) partner(s), or if the distress between the two of you is in fact the result of some psychiatric condition, it's safest to assume that you do have both problems (though not always so easy to accept—even tentatively), and follow the guidelines that follow.

There are two parts to the task—first, to find your way to an appropriate therapist (or therapists), and second, to evaluate him (or them). Suppose, for example, one of you is depressed. You'll need to find either a psychiatrist who can treat depression and also can do couples work, a psychiatrist who treats depression and works well with a therapist who does couples work, or a therapist who does couples work and works well with a psychiatrist who can treat depression. Word of mouth is often helpful, either from your family doctor, friends, family members, or the like. Professional organizations are useful—the county medical, psychiatric, or psychological associations, for example, as well as organizations dedicated to one of the major disorders. These organizations have referral services that will give you names of therapists who specialize in whatever area you need help. Home pages, Web sites, and chat groups on the Internet are rapidly becoming the gold standard for this sort of networking.

Once you have a therapist's name, you can save time and

money by speaking to him directly—if only for a few moments—and asking some questions to see if he feels right for you. Unfortunately, most therapists resist doing this—it takes up a lot of time, and often ends with the prospective patient rejecting him. And if he's well respected in his community, he's probably already had thirty or forty phone calls, faxes, and e-mail messages that day, many of which plead for a few minutes of free time.

What I'd suggest is telling the therapist (or his secretary or voice mail) that you'd like to ask a question or two before coming in, and that you're willing to pay for the time. This changes the circumstance from one demanding free time to one offering him a choice—whether to field your questions, to schedule a few minutes at some other time, to charge for the time, and so on. Some therapists will bill you for this and some won't, but most will be more willing to answer your questions, and therefore more likely to answer them more completely.

If, after fielding your questions, a therapist doesn't think he's right for you, he'll usually be happy to give you the names of colleagues he thinks are more appropriate. After all, he gets out of something he doesn't want to do, and he knows that his colleagues will appreciate the referral. If, on the other hand, you don't think he's right for you, that's your prerogative. You don't have to be apologetic. Just thank him for his time and say you'll need time to think about what you'd like to do (and then look elsewhere)—as you would in a store if you don't want to buy something but don't want to hurt the salesclerk's feelings.

Assuming you've found a psychiatrist, or a psychiatrist plus therapist, how do you decide as you meet him that he's right for you? In the first place, you can learn a good deal about him from how he answers your questions—whether he's defensive or open, whether he respects and understands the issues you raise, whether he seems flexible enough to adapt his approach to your needs, and so on. If he lets you start the consultation with your concerns (which most of us will do), you can ask right off whether he deals with both aspects of your problem (the psychiatric and the interpersonal), or has someone with whom he works to handle the things he doesn't.

Some therapists take charge in the first interview and ask so many questions that it's difficult to bring up a topic of your own.

In this case, you should interrupt him at some point to say that you'll do your best to answer his questions, but that you'd like some time before you finish for your questions. You may find, however, that he gets to all your issues and concerns on his own, and that he answers them appropriately. In that case, being directive is simply an aspect of his interviewing style. Still, if his directiveness (or any other aspect of his clinical style) makes you uncomfortable, he may not be right for you. It doesn't make sense to work with someone who makes you uncomfortable. If, regardless of his style, there simply isn't time in your first appointment for your questions, do the sort of thing I suggested. Ask if you can pay him for a few minutes for questions later—either in his office or on the phone. This may cost a few more dollars, but it can save a good deal of time, money, and discomfort by helping you avoid a person you can't work with.

What to Ask

We've seen that there are so many schools of thought about talking therapy, and so many individual approaches within each school, that choosing a therapist can feel overwhelming. It's especially difficult if you're struggling with a partner and with a psychiatric disorder that would make you feel hopeless and helpless even without added complications. Here are some specific questions that will start you out of the woods.

1. *I think I am (or my partner is) depressed (or has ADD, OCD, etc.), and that this causes problems in our relationship. Do you deal with medically treatable disorders like depression (or ADD, etc.) or cooperate with someone who can treat them?*

If he doesn't acknowledge the disorders or treatment, or can't argue knowledgeably that they're not relevant in your case, then he isn't for you. If he does treat (or collaborates with someone who treats) biologically based conditions, then you can ask about relationship issues.

2. *I think the depression (or ADD, OCD, etc.) is hurting our*

relationship, and we'd like help with that too. Can you help us with relationship issues, or work with someone who will?

It's asking a lot to have you confront an authority you barely know at a time when your (or your partner's) psyche is compromised and your relationship is shaky. Nonetheless, you'll need answers to these questions. It may be easier if you write them down first, and then read them to the doctor. Some people find it easier to ask them over the phone.

Once you ask a question, listen carefully to how the therapist responds. If he does his best to understand your concerns, fine. If he wants to know more about you and your relationship before answering, that's fine too. It's not okay, on the other hand, for him to assume a posture of superiority and devalue what you've said or the sources of what you said. Therapists do this in all kinds of ways. Some say, for example, that ADD is just a fad. This includes many psychiatrists (often in HMOs, where this attitude saves money that might otherwise be squandered on patient care). The statement is not only inaccurate, it's also dangerous, and tells you to look elsewhere. Even if he were right (which he isn't), closing off discussion so early makes no sense whatever. Even if ninety-nine percent of people who think they had ADD don't (which is not the case), you could be in the one percent, and he should find that out before dismissing your concerns about the disorder. Suppose, for example, you have the symptoms of ADD because you've been exposed to a toxic level of lead—his lofty dismissal of your concerns may prevent your getting treatment for a serious medical condition. His response also shows a glib contempt for medical research, or an unwillingness to keep up with it. Calling something like ADD a fad implies that the hundreds of researchers who consistently find it in about ten percent of children are incompetent or delusional—and this isn't likely.

It's not hard to cross people like these off your list. What's harder is if the therapist does listen but decides in only a few minutes that you're wrong about the ADD, depression, or other condition. He may, of course, be right—but you'd better make sure. There are a number of questions to ask in this situation. An especially useful one is:

3. *What symptoms would you need to see to make the diagnosis?*

If he quibbles, ask him if he knows the diagnostic criteria for the condition he's saying you don't have. If he quibbles some more, or tells you that it's inappropriate to quiz him like this, then he's telling you that he doesn't know enough about the disorder to diagnose it, or to rule it out, and that you're in the wrong office. (Don't worry about hurting his feelings in this case. If he's upset by your questions, he may think about it later and go learn something.) He may, on the other hand, say something sensible, for example, that since ADD is a lifelong condition (which you may not have known) and your symptoms come and go, it's more likely that a recurrent depression or an unusual medical condition is causing your difficulty with concentration and focus. Or he may point out that your promiscuous partner probably isn't manic because, beyond his sexual misconduct (which in itself isn't diagnostic), there aren't any signs of mania or even hypomania. In these cases, he's not being defensive; he's just doing his job—part of which is to know more about psychiatric disorders than you do.

It's most important that your therapist know the signs and symptoms of the major psychiatric disorders, whether or not he's a physician. As I've said all along, it's easy to be clever and explain away the symptoms of a biologically based disorder in terms of purely psychological factors. Unfortunately, mistaking psychiatric symptoms for psychological issues traps a great many people in lengthy and unproductive periods of talking therapy. This can also leave them trapped in troubled or inappropriate relationships or, as we'll see in a moment, out of good relationships altogether.

I'm afraid this happens quite often. This morning, for example, I was consulted by a man in his early forties I'll call Ted. His problem was that he couldn't decide which of two therapists to see. One was a psychoanalyst he'd seen for almost two years, and had made significant progress with him. All his life Ted had felt that his father's overbearing manner and persistent dissatisfaction with all his children, along with his mother's possessiveness, had been the bases of his difficulties with women. Over the course of his therapy, he learned that he'd misunderstood his father in a number of ways, and found that knowing this softened his father's negative effect substantially. He was pleased, and optimistic that the next step would be to progress regarding his mother and her influence on him.

At about this time he met a woman who insisted that he see her therapist. Ted saw him in consultation, and the therapist told him that the psychoanalytic approach simply wasn't productive—for anyone. Ted knew this wasn't true in his case, because he'd already made substantial progress with it. Nonetheless, he found himself stuck in a quandary over whether to stay with his current therapist or start treatment with the new one.

Soon he found that his inability to decide was getting him down. Fortunately, his internist noticed the drop in mood, and arranged a consultation with me. One look at Ted's expression, posture, and slowed movements made it clear that he was significantly depressed. As we reviewed the past few months, we were able to establish that his depression had begun sometime before he saw the second therapist. Thus we could conclude that Ted's indecision about therapy was actually a depressive symptom, not a blend of psychological factors. Leaving this fact out of the mix not only risked his discontinuing a productive course of treatment, but also accounted for his sinking into a serious depressive episode. And most significant for his interpersonal life, not dealing with his depression and its effects had kept him from learning that his recurring depression was very likely the major cause of his unsatisfying interpersonal life.

Let's return to evaluating a therapist. If it's clear after the questions and answers that the one you've found is open and knowledgeable about your concerns, fine. If you're not sure, asking a few more questions may clarify things. For example:

4. *Have you treated many people with my disorder?*

5. *Have you had much success?*

Again, if he quibbles, he's telling you he's not comfortable treating the disorder, and you should move on.

There's one question you'll need to ask at some point in the first interview:

6. *Are you willing to talk to my partner?*

Every therapist knows that there are both advantages and disadvantages to seeing both partners together, even if it's at separate times. If they're fighting, for example, each may try, sometimes very subtly and therefore very effectively, to recruit you to his side of a conflict. At other times you can find yourself in the position of icon—and, both in and out of your office, they waste good time discussing you, your virtues, and your quirks rather than themselves and their troubles. Sometimes one or the other fears that the therapist won't be able to maintain confidentiality—and, despite my insistence that this is easy to avoid (see Chapter Ten), it is always possible that the therapist will slip and distress one partner with something the other said. On the other hand, as I've said, there are many advantages to including both partners—so many, in fact, that I can't imagine working with a patient whose psychiatric disorder disturbs a relationship without seeing both partners.

Each therapist has to decide for himself how to handle this issue. If a therapist's approach seems too rigid for you, or not well thought out, or indicates some other problem with his approach (in your eyes), then you must consider looking elsewhere. An automatic refusal to see your partner, for example, will disqualify a number of therapists. Psychoanalysts typically refuse to see partners—though this stance may have softened a bit since my psychoanalytic days. Still, the other day I was asked to see an adolescent for depression because her sister's psychiatrist, an analyst who sees the girl for medication management only, will not see two siblings in the same family. It seems a shame when an analyst (who's especially knowledgeable about family interactions) won't see family members simultaneously, especially in a relatively uncharged setting like medication management.

Treatment Modalities

The choice of therapist, and therefore of a specific treatment approach, can make a tremendous difference in how well a patient, and his relationships, fare. In the face of so many conflicting claims of efficacy for these approaches, it's best to rely on treatment methods that are tried and true—though at the same time to keep one's mind open to new ideas. Fortunately, there are a number of well-established treatments for each of the disorders we've discussed. Though I've emphasized the use of medication, there are at least two other approaches that have been shown repeatedly to be as effective as medication for many conditions. These are behavior modification therapy and cognitive therapy. Over the last few years, a third alternative has been introduced that looks very promising. It's called EEG biofeedback or neurofeedback, and although it hasn't been tested as extensively as the classical modalities, it seems likely that before too long it will be very useful and very widely used—and in time it may be the most useful of the available treatments. I'll describe the first two approaches briefly, and then present a little more detail about neurofeedback, because it's still relatively unknown and because of (what many of us feel is) its tremendous potential.

Cognitive therapy is based on the idea that psychological functioning, and malfunctioning, are strongly dependent on a set of beliefs about oneself and the world—beliefs that are often completely subconscious. The approach was first developed by psychiatrist Aaron Beck to treat depression. He identified three beliefs as central to a person's experience of depression: (1) the world of both people and things is too difficult to negotiate, (2) I am weak and cannot cope with it, and (3) the future holds no hope for positive change in me or in the world. Beck called these beliefs the cognitive triad of depression, and believed that they form the basis of the hopelessness, helplessness, and other symptoms of depression. Many of us would not agree that the cognitive triad is the cause of depression (especially severe depression), but most would agree that Beck's ideas are very useful clinically. Treatment based on a systematic identification and reformulation of a patient's belief system has been shown to be effective in treating depressive as well as anxiety disorders. ADD, on the other hand, doesn't respond to it—though the behavioral problems and depression that typically accompany ADD probably do respond.

Behavior modification developed as an attempt to describe behavior in purely observational terms; that is, leaving out the speculative and intangible hypotheses so common in psychological theories like those of Freud or Jung. Therapists work only with the specific problematic behaviors themselves, systematically bringing these back to normal. Over the last few decades, however, behaviorists have incorporated ideas from cognitive psychology into their work, and called the resulting therapeutic hybrid cognitive behavioral therapy. Whether in its original or its cognitive form, behavioral therapy has been especially useful with anxiety disorders as well as with mood disorders. Behaviorists have devised a number of ways to treat pathological behavior in people with mental disorders, and find that nonbehavioral symptoms are resolved as well. A wide range of techniques have been developed.

A typical example is that of graded exposure in treating of phobias. In this technique a person is exposed to whatever frightens him (technically, the phobic object) in progressively larger doses, so to speak. At each level of exposure, he uses relaxation techniques at the same time as he's exposed to the phobic object. A person with a phobia of spiders, for example, may first be shown pictures of spiders—perhaps with an increasing degree of realism as the treatment proceeds. He's then exposed to increasingly realistic models of spiders, and eventually is allowed to come closer and closer to the real item. At each step he uses the relaxation techniques he's been taught to stay calm in the presence of the frightening image—and eventually in the presence of an actual spider. Underlying this technique is the assumption that a person cannot be anxious and relaxed at the same time, and that with treatment, relaxation can win out.

Neurofeedback, or EEG-based biofeedback, is based on the observation that people with attentional, mood, and other disorders have abnormal patterns of brain waves (strictly speaking, cortical electrical potentials). These are microvolt-strength electric fields generated by the brain's electrical activity, mainly from the cerebral cortex. An analysis of brain-wave patterns over the entire scalp can yield surprisingly accurate diagnostic impressions and suggestions for treatment. As naive as it sounds, the technique works by training a patient to adjust the pattern of his brain waves toward normal.

Practically, the method works by attaching electrodes to points on the scalp and feeding the signals to an EEG (electroencephalograph) machine. The machine sends the signal to a computer, which determined how close the person's patterns are to those of people without the disorder. The computer then runs a game that allows the person to adjust his patterns toward normal. A typical game resembles the Pac-man computer game. It's programmed so that the closer the patient's brain-wave pattern approaches the normal pattern (that of patients without whatever condition is being treated), the faster the Pac-man figure moves through his mazes. The patient tries to move the figure on the screen as rapidly as possible. Thus, what he's doing is (somehow) adjusting his brain-wave patterns so that they approach the normal patterns—and learning how to do this by using the feedback of how fast Pac-man moves. [What's probably happening is that adjusting the brain waves adjusts the brain states (that generate the abnormal brain-wave patterns) toward normal. This in turn adjusts the activity at the synapses back to normal (neurotransmitter release, receptor characteristics, and so on). Doing this over a long enough time makes the changes permanent—like the changes in synaptic activity in motor circuits when you learn, through practice, a motor skill like typing or riding a bicycle (which, of course, are permanently acquired).]

If this process is carried out long enough (for about a half hour at a time), and for enough times (about forty), the EEG patterns stabilize much closer to normal—and, in a significant number of cases, the disorder clears up, often for long periods of time. This appeals to many patients who won't accept the idea of medication, can't endure their side effects, and so on.

As with the introduction of any new technique, there's great controversy raging about the validity and efficacy of neurofeedback—the loudest, as usual, from those who are the most ignorant of its characteristics or results. Nonetheless, to my eye, an impressive body of both clinical success and scientific documentation is accumulating to suggest that the technique stands on firm scientific ground and is very effective for a range of psychiatric disorders. The best-documented studies of neurofeedback are with ADD. The most significant findings are (1) that EEG patterns are an easy and reliable way to diagnose ADD, and (2) that treatment, at least for children and probably for adults, seems to persist over long periods after a course of treatment is completed. (People often ask how patients with ADD can sit still long enough for the technique to work. The answer is the same as to the question of how so many people with ADD do such good computer-related work: through a combination of their capacity to hyperfocus and of the "adrenaline rush" of doing something interesting and important.)

If these findings are validated, the implications are staggering. We could, for example, test all first-graders, and treat the ones who test positive for ADD—thereby sparing some ten percent of the population the demoralizing experiences I detailed in Chapter Three. Likewise, we could test prisoners and treat them for it—thereby rehabilitating a tremendous number of people who, without this technique are unlikely ever to set aside their criminal activities. This would yield enormous benefits—estimates are that up to eighty percent of people in jails and prisons have ADD. The increased productivity of the inmates when released, the decreased cost of treating, incarcerating, and cleaning up after them would rival, if not far outstrip, the gains from the introduction of psychotropic medication.

On a more modest level, the availability of neurofeedback for psychiatric conditions gives us greater flexibility in treating them. Around ten to twenty percent of patients don't respond well to medication, and about the same percentage don't respond to neurofeedback—but they aren't the same group. Thus, if treatment with medication isn't working, a referral to a neurofeedback therapist can be very useful (and vice versa).

There are two organizations that you can contact for more information and for referral to therapists who practice neurofeedback. They are:

Society for the Study of Neuronal Regulation
4600 Post Oak Place, Suite 301
Houston, Texas 77027
1-713-552-0091

Biofeedback Certification Institute of America
10200 W. 45th Ave., Suite 304
Wheat Ridge, Colorado 80033-2840
1-303-420-2902

CHAPTER 10

How to Use a Psychiatrist

Getting There

There are a number of ways you can get to a psychiatrist's office. In the (good old) days before managed care, an internist, friend, or family member gave you a doctor's name, you called him, and set up an appointment. This still happens, especially for a consultation, a second opinion, or for medication management only. These situations cost less than seeing him on an ongoing basis, and are therefore more affordable even without help from an insurance company. In my experience, this sort of referral works the best. It's comforting when someone who knows you well gives you the name of the doctor he thinks is the best for you rather than picking a doctor out of the phone book or from an insurance company list. The other time-tested way to a psychiatrist's office is for a nonmedical therapist to send you for consultation with someone he thinks will be good for you. Here again the choice is based on what someone who knows you thinks you need, and there's the added advantage that he's probably chosen someone he likes to work with. If you're not sure about this, ask him.

If the present trends in managed care continue, however, referrals like these may become a thing of the past. Increasingly, referrals are made by managed care companies—often by clerks or secretaries who choose a psychiatrist (or other specialist) from a list, authorize a (small) number of visits, and send you and the doctor a pound or so of paperwork. The choice, from what I can tell, has a lot to do with who's next on the list, or who returns his calls the quickest, and not enough to do with matching up a patient with the psychiatrist who seems best for him. Both doctor and patient can feel as if they're interchangeable parts snapped or hinged together in the grand machine of the insurance industry— and they very often are.

From what I've seen, patients linking up with psychiatrists this way don't do as well as they did with the old ways. They miss appointments more frequently (especially the first), do not cooperate as well, and are less persistent when treatment isn't going so well—all things you'd expect when there isn't a personal connection between doctor and patient built in from the start. It's also harder for the doctor to connect with his patient. Try as you might, your enthusiasm fades when you have to justify, on paper and in person, your treatment plans every five or six sessions to case managers who don't have your training and experience— and when you're paid a reduced fee for this privilege. Fortunately, the managers I've worked with so far strike me as quite concerned about the patient's welfare, often to the point of being very effective advocates. But I worry that this, too, will become old-fashioned, and that referral and treatment planning will be guided purely by concerns of maximizing profit for the companies.

I belabor all this to warn you that new trends in mental health delivery are starting to get in the way of good care—and that you'll have to watch all this very carefully. If your managed care company does get you good medical and mental health care, stay with it—but keep your eyes open for changes for the worse. If it is difficult for you to get the right psychiatrist, for example, you may have to take matters into your own hands and consult someone you think is best for you—even if you have to pay for it yourself. Considering all that's at stake, the cost of a psychiatric consultation isn't really that high. It's, well, about half as much as I just paid the vet to remove a two-centimeter lump from the dog's hind leg (it turned out to be benign). All in all, the cost (a mere half-lump) is a pretty solid investment in your mental well-being and in the quality of your relationships. I don't use this homey example to trivialize the expense—when you're suffering from both a psychiatric disorder and a strained relationship, any investment of time and money feels too costly. But I know how useful a timely consultation with the right person can be—and what an emotional boost it is to take matters into your own hands and make something good happen.

Being There

Since we're dealing with problems within a relationship, both partners need to be included in the work. Sometimes it's best to start with one person (usually the one with the disorder), and then bring in the other later. At other times it's best for both partners to start together. Whenever either speaks alone with the therapist, however, questions about confidentiality usually come up. People ask, for example, if they see the therapist alone, and then bring in their partner (or vice versa), will the doctor tell him things I don't want her to know—like about my affair, or that I've already seen a divorce attorney?

The answer is no. Confidentiality laws differ from state to state, but the common denominator (and common sense) is that your therapist can't tell anyone what you've said unless you tell him to. The only exceptions are when suicide or homicide seem sufficiently likely. In these circumstances he must break confidentiality to protect you or a possible victim. People also wonder if it's possible for the therapist to keep straight who said what when he sees the partners at different times, so that he doesn't inadvertently tell someone something he shouldn't. I reassure them that this isn't hard to do: You simply make it a rule never to say anything secondhand—no matter how harmless it seems.

Still, it's easiest for the doctor if your partner is included from the start. Including a partner early has other advantages. The therapist can explain that you (or your partner) are suffering from a mental disorder with a biochemical basis—and that you're not, as many partners fear, being manipulative or malingering, but rather that you're depressed and will get better. Or that you're not lazy or irresponsible or stupid—but have ADD and will get better. Likewise with obsessions, compulsions, phobias, and panic attacks. These insights can greatly relieve a partner. The therapist can then explain how a partner can help with the recovery process—by doing what helps and avoiding what gets in the way. For example, the partner's acceptance goes a long way toward helping someone recover from a depression. On the other hand, anyone will become depressed, or more depressed, if his partner demands that he change a number of unchangeable things—like his temperament or his interests. For a phobic, how well his partner can set aside the role of his protector and become a facilitator of his autonomy goes a long way toward getting him past his phobia.

Thus, for each disorder the doctor can help the partner do what helps and avoid what hinders. At the same time, he can teach both partners how the disorder is disrupting communication. He can show you how depression makes you think your partner is more critical than he is, how ADD makes you miss much of what he says and then fill in the gaps with your imagination, or how anxiety makes you distort or censor whatever he says.

A partner's participation also lends objectivity to assessing someone's clinical progress—especially with depression. We've seen, for example, that as a patient starts to recover from depression, he can be the last to know it. Easily observed signs of depression like sad facial expression, stooped posture, or a loss of animation in speech and activity usually respond sooner than more subjective symptoms like low self-esteem, a sense of hopelessness, or guilt. Thus, it's quite common that at the second appointment the partner reports significant improvement, while the person himself denies it. In this case, raising the antidepressant dose, or simply waiting a few days as it becomes fully effective, usually leads to improvement in the subjective symptoms so that the person can feel his progress. This can be critical, because without the partner's objectivity it's easy for both therapist and patient to miss early or subtle signs of improvement. This can lead to giving up on a medication that would have started to resolve the depression if they'd given it a little longer.

All this praise of cooperation having been noted, let's return to the details of treatment and how to make the best use of it.

Therapeutic Options

To illustrate what you can expect in a psychiatrist's office, I'll present a typical consultation. I'll describe what I do in my office, of course, but I think it's typical of what happens in most cases.

Suppose the referral has been made, decisions about including a partner, cooperating with another therapist, and other details have been made. You, the prospective patient, now meet me, the doctor. If both partners have come, I let whoever's identified himself as the patient come into the office alone for our first meeting or with his partner. If neither of them is labeled the "problem partner," I have both come in from the start. Questions about confidentiality, fees, and other details often come up early. Handling details like these at the beginning gives all of us time to feel comfortable with one another and with the setting, so that we can move on to the problem issues.

The identified patient or partner (or both) then tells his story. As I listen to them, I start to get a sense of their personalities, and begin to collect (in my head, not aloud) signs and symptoms of any psychiatric disorders I suspect. Over time I'll organize what I've understood into a working diagnosis for each of them— though I won't necessarily be able to do this on the first visit. I also try to get a sense of their relationship, and how personal or psychiatric problems affect it. If the relationship isn't in trouble, most of our attention is taken up with reaching a diagnosis and treatment options. If the relationship is in trouble, we address this right off the bat. Over the first thirty or forty minutes, then, I begin to get an idea of the partners' personality styles, and whether there were psychological problems in the past. I also try to understand the psychiatric, medical, family, social, and drug history for whichever partner (or both) is likely to need treatment. I know that this must sound like a lot to learn in such a short time, but you'd be amazed how much a person in distress can say in a half hour. I summarize my impressions to make sure we're all on the same page, and answer any questions they have to that point.

To give as palpable an impression as possible, I'll introduce Kim and Jason, a pair whose treatment illuminates most of what I'm presenting here.

Kim and Jason came to my office by referral from the employee assistance program at Kim's work. Her supervisor had been concerned that for some weeks she hadn't been able to concentrate on her work, and when he mentioned this, she flew into a rage. Jason came along, they told me, only for moral support. At first glance there didn't seem to be much amiss about Kim. She was in her early thirties, pretty, and nicely dressed. As she talked, though, she had a tentativeness and timidity, as if she were asking for my approval but didn't feel that I'd give it. I asked her about this as tactfully as I could, and she agreed that, yes, she did feel this way, and had throughout her life. It was worse now though. She was losing confidence in her ability to work, to think clearly, and to attract or satisfy Jason sexually.

At work these feelings of insecurity made her afraid to accept challenging assignments—she was sure she'd do them wrong and be reprimanded. This worry tormented her continuously, especially in the middle of the night. She awoke invariably at three or four A.M., and usually could not fall back to sleep. Thus she was sleepy all day—a situation that made concentration on her work almost impossible. She was puzzled that despite all this, from time to time she had the energy to explode into a rage whenever she felt that someone criticized her too unfairly. She thought (correctly, I think) that because of her extreme sensitivity to criticism, she lashed out so that no one would dare criticize her twice. Though her mood was especially low now, it had been low all throughout her life. She'd had a lifelong tendency to self-doubt and pessimism, along with a vulnerability to depression at times of separations or loss.

I watched Jason as Kim talked. At first he watched and listened intensely, but more and more his gaze wandered off—sometimes out the window, sometimes at the books on the shelves, sometimes at me—all the while fidgeting in his chair and bouncing his legs. When I finished talking with Kim, I asked Jason about his behavior. He said that he'd always been fidgety. It was hard for him to focus well enough to carry on a long conversation, read a long book, or finish a complex task. This had limited his career, but he'd accepted that it meant he wasn't as smart as others. Their greater intelligence, he imagined, let them listen, read, and sit still long enough to get things done.

By this time it seemed most likely that Kim was in a depressive episode superimposed on a chronic depression, and that Jason was a victim of ADD. There were, however, a number of other possibilities for Kim's problems including medical ones masquerading as psychiatric ones. There wasn't much uncertainty about Jason's condition. I told Kim that I'd like to work with her internist to rule out any medical cause for her troubles (and mentioned a few relatively benign conditions, like anemia or hypoglycemia). Then I shared my initial impressions and answered a few questions. Throughout the discussion neither Kim nor Jason had complained about the relationship—and in fact each said several times how supportive it was. It seemed unlikely that the combination of depression and ADD didn't make at least some trouble between them, but discretion seemed the better part of valor at that point.

After this initial meeting, the next step is to discuss treatment options. If one of the partners is depressed, like Kim, I explain that medication, cognitive therapy, and neurofeedback (or a combination of these) are useful for depression, describe each approach, and see what the partners preferences are. If one of them has ADD, like Jason, I explain about medication or neurofeedback—and so on through the syndromes. Around this time (sometimes earlier) one or the other partner expresses reluctance about treatment. I make sure we discuss the reluctance in as much detail as desired. If a patient prefers a particular treatment approach, and his choice seems reasonable, I usually agree and tell him what we need to do to get started. If I don't think the patient's preferences or the reasons behind them are sound, I tell him that, and we try to work through the differences in our points of view. I tell patients that I prescribe medication and do individual and couples therapy, but that I don't do cognitive or behavior treatments or neurofeedback. If they prefer one of the treatments I don't do, I refer them to someone who does.

At the point of planning treatment, things bogged down. Kim had vigorous reservations about medication: I should be able to do it myself, I don't want to pollute my body with artificial substances, I worry the medications are addictive, and so on through my list of resistances in Chapter Eight and beyond. By the time she'd articulated all these reservations, the session was nearly over. I took a few minutes to tell Jason about the treatment options for ADD. He said he'd think about it for a week or so. We scheduled a follow-up appointment for the next week to continue our discussion of treatment.

For several sessions, Kim stuck to her guns, while Jason said he'd like to try a course of medication for his ADD. I suggested psychotherapy to Kim for everything that was bothering her. I sent her to a therapist who was knowledgeable about depression, relationship issues, and about the resistances to taking medication.

Unlike Kim, most people come to my office hoping that psychiatric medication will help them. Some have already used medication or know about it from friends or reading, and are eager to begin. In many cases whoever has referred them to me has already prepared them that I might recommend medication. Others have a great deal of ambivalence and a number of questions and challenges. If I can answer their concerns and there's enough time, I prescribe one of the psychotropic medications at the end of the session, and give instructions about how to take them, what to expect about side effects, when and how to call me, and so on. Sometimes the situation is so complex, or the patient has so many questions or so much hesitation, there isn't time to prescribe anything. In these cases we schedule some later time (sometimes on the phone) to work out the details of starting medication.

Practical Details of Taking Medication

Sometime during the first appointment I tell my patient(s) an absolute essential for doing psychiatry: Both doctor and patient have to be persistent. In the majority of cases in which the first or second medication works well, you won't need much persistence. In twenty or thirty percent of cases, though, things don't go so easily. There's either no beneficial effect with the first few medications you try, or there are intolerable side effects, or both. At that point you will need persistence. If the first, or even the first several medications don't do the job, don't assume that you're using the wrong family of medications (antidepressants, anti-anxiety medications etc.) or that your doctor's diagnosis isn't correct. It probably means that you haven't found the particular medication that is right for you yet. You have to try several medications, or combinations of medications, and do this in a logical sequence. It's not unusual to try five or more medications before finding one (or a combination of several) to get a good result.

Twenty years ago most psychiatrists thought that using combinations of medications was unsophisticated. It was called "polypharmacy," and generally looked down on—especially by academic psychiatrists (who didn't treat many patients). Looking back, it's hard to understand how anyone (even academics) could expect a single compound to fix anyone's brain, with its billions of cells, hundreds of neurotransmitters, and (probably) dozens of receptor types for each of these. To me the remarkable thing is that in most cases one medication does do the job. But in more difficult cases, the trials and errors are frustrating to both doctor and patient, and after a while you feel like mad scientist and guinea pig. But you're not—the majority of patients with the conditions we've studied do respond within a few weeks or at most within a few months of starting treatment. This is especially likely when any one of the medications makes even a small change for the better over the first few weeks. Once this happens, you can almost always find a medication or combination of medications that resolve the symptoms.

Jason's treatment for ADD was a moderately complex case, and involved adjustments and combinations of medications. At first we tried Ritalin—a standard first choice for ADD. At a moderate dose he found significant improvement in his fidgeting and leg bouncing, and his concentration was better in reading and conversations. Still, he felt that there was room for improvement. The changes with Ritalin had made his thinking sufficiently clear for him to see that other people could still think and focus better than he could. The clearheadedness from Ritalin had also brought the realization that others weren't smarter or better than he was, but, rather, they could focus and sit still longer. Unfortunately, we couldn't raise his dose because this caused shakiness and insomnia as side effects. Therefore, we tried Dexedrine, another standard choice for ADD, especially in adults. We lowered the Ritalin dose as we ramped up the Dexedrine dose. When we reached the point of using only Dexedrine, Jason felt almost exactly as he had on Ritalin alone. As he thought back, though, it seemed that he had felt best when the doses of each were equal. His thinking was clearest and most organized, he said, and he could sit still for the longest periods, read or concentrate the best, and follow discussions the best.

Using this combination of medications upsets a lot of people, especially pharmacists and other psychiatrists reviewing (or commenting about) your work. On paper the two medications do the same thing, they argue, so why mix them? They worry that Dexedrine can be addictive, but it's almost never addictive at appropriate doses for people with ADD. They also worry that side effects will be worse for the combinations than for a double dose of either. None of this worry makes much sense—the combinations work and the side effects of the two usually aren't greater than the sum of each alone.

Side Effects: Anything Can Cause Anything

Managing side effects can be difficult. Though in general they've become less troublesome with the newer generations of medication, they're still a major headache to both doctor and patient (sometimes quite literally). Fortunately, all side effects are reversible (the one exception is discussed momentarily)— that is, they go away when the medication is discontinued. In addition, they usually fade with time and when the medication dose is lowered. Still, the details are complex. Some side effects are dose related, and some aren't. Some tend to persist over long periods, and others tend to fade rapidly. And, of course, it's all different for each patient. Further, for any side effect of any particular medication (say, sedation from an antidepressant) there are people who experience the exact opposite effect (excitement or insomnia from the same antidepressant). The one exception to the reversibility of side effects is a set of persistent movement disorders (mainly tardive dyskinesia) that follows long-term use of antipsychotic medication. Fortunately, the antipsychotics are almost never used with the conditions discussed in this book.

Until the last decade or so, the side effects of many psychiatric medications were not only irritating, they were dangerous as well. The first group of antidepressants introduced, the tricyclics, had serious cardiac effects. The monamine oxidase inhibitors, the second class of antidepressants introduced, can cause serious drops in blood pressure, and dangerous elevations in blood pressure if taken with certain foods and medications. The older antianxiety agents (especially the barbiturates) are addictive and at high doses cause respiratory suppression. Unfortunately, the serious effects were not uncommon, and were especially dangerous in overdoses. All this made treating suicidal patients especially problematic because both the antidepressants and antianxiety agents could be used in a suicide attempt—and often were.

Fortunately, the more recently introduced medications are almost entirely free of the more dangerous side effects. The newer antidepressants, starting with the release of Prozac in 1988, are generally free of cardiac effects, and the newer antianxiety medications are free of respiratory suppression. The side effects of both most often decrease in severity, if not disappear completely, over the first few days or weeks of treatment. These include nausea with Prozac and other new antidepressants and sedation with the antianxiety agents. On the other hand, headaches, sleep disturbances, and disturbances in libido or orgastic capacity with the newer antidepressants can take months to resolve, and sometimes persist over long periods. In these cases, a change to a different medication is usually necessary. Changing to a different medication in the same class, or to a different class of medication, often avoids the side effects but retains the therapeutic effects. Since there are a number of classes of medication and a number of medications in each class, this approach is almost always available. Another approach is changing to neurofeedback, which I'll discuss in a moment.

Problems with side effects can be minimized by starting with very low doses and raising them slowly. Usually this doesn't diminish the effectiveness of the medication. If a side effect becomes a problem during the ramp-up, it helps to lower the dose back to what it was before the side effect appeared, and then leave it there for a week or so. By this time the dose can usually be ramped back up without the side effect recurring. Sometimes, in fact, the therapeutic effect "kicks in" at the lower dose after a week or so, and the dose doesn't need to be raised.

You can read the company's package insert for a complete list of side effects of any medication. However, these inserts are so detailed and contain so many potentially dangerous, though very rare, effects that they frighten some patients. All medical conditions that arise in subjects taking the medication in drug studies—including many conditions that are most likely unrelated to the medication being tested—must be reported. You may therefore want to ask your doctor if there are any serious side effects, even if rare, and if so, how rare.

This last point is important. Many doctors handle statistical issues in a careless way, unfortunately. When he was deciding what to do with a bump on my thyroid, for example, my endocrinologist said he was inclined not to do a follow-up biopsy because the chance of its being malignant was so small. How small? Around two percent. I didn't think that one out of fifty was so small, so we biopsied it. It was benign—but for every fiftieth patient, it isn't. Knowing the actual percentages is absolutely necessary in order to make an informed decision about medication (or anything else medical).

One final point. Whether or not the package insert lists a certain side effect for a particular medication, it's never safe to rule out any medication as the source of any side effect. The best rule of thumb is that any medication can cause any side effect. Lists and percentages are best used as guides to which medications are the most likely culprits. Sometimes the only way to know if a particular medication is causing a particular side effect is to raise or lower the dose, and see how this affects the offending symptom.

As a Medication Begins to Work

Medications vary in how soon they act, how long they act, how long to reach peak activity, and so on. Stimulants like Dexedrine or Ritalin and antianxiety medications like Valium or Xanax can take effect within a half hour to an hour. Especially with children and young adults, you can see a resolution of symptoms after one dose (though you have to continue taking it to maintain the effect). Mood stabilizers like lithium carbonate or Tegretol can take a week or longer to affect a patient's mood. With antidepressants and antipsychotics, different symptoms respond at different times. Antipsychotics typically produce sedation and control agitation in a matter of hours, but can take days to weeks to affect psychotic symptoms like disorganized thought, chaotic behavior, hallucinations, or delusions.

With antidepressants, the onset of sedation from the medication (if it appears) is rapid, and a good night's sleep often follows the first dose. The symptoms of agitation and irritability tend to respond in a matter of days. If your doctor was trained like I was, he'll tell you that it takes two weeks or more for an antidepressant effect to appear. However, I have found that patients often felt much better within a day or two. Thus, if your response to an antidepressant is this rapid, it's most likely real (and will persist) and not a placebo effect, as many people will insist. There are good physiological reasons that different people take different periods of time to respond to an antidepressant, and that some people can respond within a matter of days. Besides, the placebo effect isn't very strong in people who are depressed. (The endorphin system, which probably mediates placebo effects, doesn't function so well in depressed patients.)

A few other distressing things can happen over the first few days of treatment. One is called early worsening—symptoms get worse for the first few days of antidepressant treatment. If the worsening of symptoms doesn't reach an intolerable level, persevering for a few days will often bring a therapeutic effect. The opposite effect can be just as distressing—a patient feels wonderful for the first few days, and then the feeling disappears. As with early worsening, it pays to persevere—raising the dose usually recaptures the antidepressant effect (as I said in Chapter Nine, the brain and liver have probably conspired to lower blood levels). Most patients say, however, that the wonderful feeling of the first few days never quite returns.

It's just as well. The goal of treatment is to return a person to a state of normality, not of wonderfulness. A chronic sense of wonderfulness is rarely a realistic response to the world as it is—

and can lead to maladaptive passive responses to the daily sea of troubles that we're better off taking on actively.

If Medication Doesn't Work

Sometimes nothing you try works. For each psychiatric disorder there are a number of standard procedures for dealing with these so-called treatment-resistant cases—running through a wider range of medication, combining medications, and so on. There are dozens of textbooks, review articles, and seminars available to teach your doctor how to do this. Your job is to be sure he has a rational plan for doing it.

If the two of you have run through the full set of rational approaches to your case, your doctor will have to rule out any medical condition underlying the psychiatric symptoms that he may have missed (or not thought of) earlier. He may want to start the process by ordering some medical tests himself, and if he doesn't uncover anything, to use a medical consultant experienced in the psychiatric manifestations of medical disorders. Or he may want to involve a consultant from the start. If all this doesn't turn up anything, your doctor should consider a psychiatric consultation by someone with special expertise in the area of your difficulties—for example, one at the psychiatry department at the nearest medical school. Some doctors prefer to get the psychiatric consultation first, and the medical consult later.

As these evaluations are going on, you, your partner, and the psychiatrist need to raise the question of whether there are psychological factors you haven't considered making the condition treatment resistant. Sometimes this involves a partner who's subtly undermining progress—uncaring or neglectful partners, for example, make depression worse, and a good deal of progress will follow separation from such a person (or from helping him to become more appropriately caretaking). Sometimes a hidden psychological issue is getting in the way. Some people need to suffer to feel valuable, others think their partners will leave them if they're not impaired, and so on. If you have both a therapist and a psychiatrist, their collaboration can be very useful in unclogging these psychological bottlenecks.

* * *

Unfortunately, some cases simply don't respond to medication, with or without ongoing psychotherapy (it may be that the right medication hasn't been synthesized yet). In these cases, other modalities such as cognitive therapy or behavior modification may take care of the problems. Neurofeedback is also a viable alternative, and in many cases is a reasonable first choice. ADD, OCD, and depression seem especially responsive to it. I've sent several of my most frustratingly resistant patients to neurofeedback therapists, and the results have been very impressive. I imagine that with time, neurofeedback will be able to do anything that medication can do—especially as academic psychiatrists and neurophysiologists become more interested in the technique.

CHAPTER 11

Potential Problems and Pitfalls

There's many a slip 'twixt cup and lip. In this final chapter I'll list a number of setbacks and complications that come up when treating partners in a troubled relationship.

Will Treating One of Us Ruin the Relationship?

As I've said all along, relationships almost always do better after one or both partners is treated for a psychiatric disorder. In my experience, it's rare for psychiatric treatment to unsettle a stable relationship—I can recall only one example. It's very common, on the other hand, for the fear of this outcome to keep a couple out of treatment. (All this is different from what happens in couples therapy generally. There couples often do separate because it was their agenda in the first place—though they weren't aware of this at first.) The one example I can recall was that of a depressed young woman married to an unusually controlling man. As she began to recover, he feared a loss of control over her, and tried ever more firmly and often unkindly to regain control of her activities, opinions, attitudes, and so on. This, of course, served only to drive her away.

As I said, the fear of psychiatric treatment destabilizing a relationship is much more common than the actuality. Sometimes, as we've just seen, the fear is about losing control of a partner if he gets better. Another is the zero-sum-game assumption: The better you do, the worse I do, and vice versa. These patterns are childish—in fact, they're normal in children from about age two to four.

To return to the case we've been following, Kim persisted in individual psychotherapy and Jason continued to consolidate gains from his medication regimen. As time went on, the issues underlying Kim's resistance to medication became much clearer. Jason's ADD had limited him both personally and professionally. He was an unusually talented engineer, but at thirty-five he couldn't advance in his company because of his interpersonal awkwardness. Thirty-five years of frustration had left him increasingly discouraged about his career and about himself. His self-esteem had been demolished by his ADD and its consequences. As the medication cleared up his thinking, however, he began to understand that he'd been using his relationship with Kim to bolster his low self-esteem.

This circumstance took its toll on Kim. She couldn't have put it into words, but she had sensed that Jason needed her to be depressed in order to feel better, by comparison, about himself (the zero-sum-game assumption). She feared, subliminally, that if she were to get better, Jason would lose interest in her. Thus, the problem wasn't that she didn't believe in medication, but that she believed in it too much—she felt that it would work and therefore make trouble for the marriage.

As Jason got better, however, everything changed. For one thing, he felt so much better about himself that he didn't need to bolster himself at Kim's expense. Also, since he now began to advance in his career, he was in a position that involved increased socializing. He wanted Kim to be as lively and lovable as she could in order to share in his new social circumstances. Once Jason could articulate this, Kim, with the help of her psychotherapist, started to understand how she'd been clinging to her depression—and how pointless it was to feel bad now. Thus she started antidepressant medication, and the combination of psychotherapy and medication soon freed her from both her current depressive episode and from her chronic dysthymia.

Adjustment of Dosage

I said in the last chapter that after an initial period of improvement, a medication sometimes seems to lose its effect. What happens is that the liver has begun to process (and therefore excrete) the medication more efficiently, and probably that the brain has begun to accommodate its effects. Simply raising the dose usually brings back the initial improvement. It's important, therefore, not to give up on a medication if it seems to wear off after a few weeks or months. It's also important to know that whenever a new medication is added, the blood level of every other medication is likely to change—sometimes to a significant degree. Thus it's important to watch for changes in their effects. If you're on a medication for high blood pressure, for example, you need periodically to check your pressure after you add an antidepressant—even though in itself the antidepressant doesn't affect blood pressure. For this reason it's also important to let every doctor you see know about *all* the medications you're taking.

I emphasize this point because many people are tempted not to tell their family doctors or other specialists about psychiatric medications, sometimes out of embarrassment, sometimes out of fear that insurance companies and other agencies will learn about their psychiatric difficulties. This is a serious mistake because, as we've seen, adding a new medication changes the blood levels of other medications. Tegretol, for example, can lower levels eightfold or more, and Prozac can raise them up as much as fourfold, to list only two examples. Whenever you add a new medication, then, be sure to ask your pharmacist and your psychiatrist about drug interactions, and tell any other doctor you see about the new medications. To be safe you should also check the package insert or the *Physician's Desk Reference* yourself for drug interactions—even if you need a microscope to read the tiny print.

People Who Feel Better Feeling Worse

Every psychiatrist has had patients who respond to medications, particularly antidepressants, in an especially exasperating way. For each of several medications, there's an initially good response, but after a few weeks or so the effect wears off and can't be recovered by changing the dose. Either there's no effect, no matter how much the dose is raised, or side effects set in at higher doses. At the same time, the patients seem to do anything and everything to interfere with their treatment—they miss appointments, come at the wrong time, stop their medications without telling you, take the wrong dose or the wrong medication, and so on. And then, to add insult to inefficiency, after a few maddening weeks or months of this they tell you it's all your fault, and then go see someone else—who, they make sure, knows what an awful doctor you are.

Why would a person act like this? The behavior (to stay with psychology for the moment) is terribly self-defeating, but like most self-defeating behavior, there's a hidden payoff. In this case it's the gratification of feeling superior to the therapist, who, in spite of his knowing better, is made to feel bumbling and ineffective.

We've seen throughout the book that people will do absolutely anything to feel good about themselves, including, in this case, keeping themselves depressed or otherwise emotionally impaired in order that their self-proclaimed victimhood continues to make them feel special. The patient feels superior to those around him, who have proven themselves inferior by letting him down so consistently. At the same time, he reaps the sadistic gratification of punishing everyone around him for disappointing him (here, by not making him better) by making them listen to endless complaints and other manifestations of depression that are hard to be around for very long. I'm aware that this interpretation, though it's been canonized into dogma in a number of classic psychoanalytic works, is speculative. Nonetheless, it's hard to concoct a better explanation for such a self-defeating approach to life—at least in terms of purely psychological forces.

In fairness to these people, the process probably goes beyond just their psychology. After watching a number of these patients go through almost identical maneuvers, you start to believe that there must be a biological component to such behavior—that their brains, at a more fundamental level than psychology, are also defeating the effects of the medication. If a patient's brain can quash the positive effects of an antidepressant, it seems likely that it can also quash any natural good feelings that threaten to overcome the depression—as a built-in response to these good feelings or moods. It's as if such a person has a self-regulating system set at a depressed baseline. Ongoing good feelings from personal or career success, the usual sources of happiness and self-esteem, aren't available to these people. For them the prime directive to feel good about themselves can be satisfied only by proclaiming themselves better than others. To this end they inflate their own self-esteem by deflating that of others—for example, by defeating them in the sort of confrontation they inflict on their psychiatrists. It seems paradoxical to sacrifice feeling good in order to be able to feel good about oneself, but, as I said, this is the way it works.

These psychological and biological explanations are really only two ways of saying the same thing, that this is a group of people who are committed, both by inclination and by brain chemistry, to defeat any attempt to make them happy. If you've brought your partner to a psychiatrist's office, and misadventures like these ensue, consider whether he's one of the people I'm describing. If you decide the answer is yes, get some good professional help dealing with what you've gotten yourself into—and possibly by getting yourself out of it.

Before ending this section I should distinguish the people I've just described from a group who at first seem similar but aren't. These are the guilt-ridden workaholics, exercise fanatics, and other people who need to abuse themselves mentally or physically in order to feel worthwhile. They feel a constant urge to accomplishment, and can't relax until they've run their daily marathon, written their weekly five chapters, or carried out some other Herculean task. At other times they punish themselves by going without luxuries or even simple comforts. They usually wish they could avoid their labors or set aside their stoicism and spend time more comfortably with friends or family, but they can't.

These are the dentists, doctors, or lawyers who take on far too many cases to let them pursue hobbies, read novels, or sometimes even see their families more than a few minutes a day. They're the coaches who eat, sleep, and drink their sport so completely and so continuously that nothing else matters—in season or out. Some of them are dysthymic, and wear themselves out like this to counter the toll chronic depression takes on their self-esteem.

The litmus test for distinguishing the groups, based on their most fundamental difference, is how they relate to others. A member of the first group uses other people to feel good about himself. He builds his self-esteem at other people's expense, including, as we've seen, his psychiatrist. Likewise, he needs other people as an audience for his complaints about how badly other people treat him—thereby making himself seem, in the eyes of his audience (he presumes), superior to those he defeats or maneuvers into abusing them.

A member of the second group, a guilty workaholic, on the other hand, doesn't involve others in his struggles—these take place only in his mind. In Freudian terms, the struggle is wholly internal, between the superego and ego, not between him and some other person. Freud used the term ego for the business end of the mind—the part that thinks, feels, learns, remembers, initiates behavior, and so on. The superego is the part of the mind that comments on and criticizes what the ego does. The superego, you'll recall, has both conscious and subconscious aspects. The part we're aware of is the conscience—the inner voice we hear telling us to behave ourselves (or to excel or accomplish). The part of the superego, however, that's out of awareness (unconscious, in Freud's lexicon) can induce guilt, a diffuse feeling of doing wrong or being wrong. As I said, the person in the second group isn't trying to feel superior to anyone—he's just trying to avoid this powerful, if subliminal, sense of guilt by bribing his superego with achievements or deprivations.

Once you've met them, it isn't as difficult to distinguish members of these groups as it may sound on paper. Someone in the first group diagnoses himself by how he affects you—the skirmishes and entanglements, complaints and gossipiness. Because of all this, people in this group usually aren't very successful with others, either in relationships or in their careers. Members of the second group, on the other hand, tend to be successful in their careers, largely because they're so driven to do well. Unlike the first group, they don't challenge or manipulate other people with their psychological problems. Unfortunately, if the problems are intense or pervasive enough, their self-containment makes problems of its own in relationships by isolating the workaholic and in extreme cases making him the stereotypic self-absorbed introvert who can't turn his attention outward to start or maintain a good relationship. If his drivenness is the result of a chronic depression, he's Chapter Seven's mimic of the very neurotic whose depression locks him out of relationships altogether.

But My Cousin's Girlfriend's Grandmother Says . . .

Everyone's an expert on psychology and psychiatry. Consequently, you're going to hear a great many opinions about what you and your psychiatrist are doing. A woman in the line with her at the pharmacy, for example, told one of my patients that two hundred milligrams of Zoloft was too much. Another patient's girlfriend read in the *PDR* that the Klonopin I'd prescribed for his panic disorder is really for seizure disorders in children, and suggested he change to her psychiatrist, who presumably would not have given such a stupid prescription. A third was told by her pharmacist that the combination of Prozac and Desyrel was a bad idea and he didn't want to fill the prescription.

To their credit, all three patients had the good sense, and courtesy, to ask me about what they'd heard—and felt better when I could reassure them. Two hundred milligrams of Zoloft, I told the first patient, is in fact the upper limit suggested by the manufacturer. I reminded her that lower doses hadn't been effective, and that her present blood level was in the lower half of the therapeutic range. I explained to the second patient that Klonopin and many other psychiatric medications are routinely prescribed in a so-called "off-label" manner—that is, for uses not explicitly mentioned in the package insert. This is because research and clinical experience have shown that they're useful in ways other than originally intended. Since psychiatric research has established these uses as valid, pharmaceutical firms don't need to spend the half billion or so dollars it would take to get the FDA to formally approve the new treatments. Finally, I pointed out to the third patient that using Prozac and Desyrel together is perfectly rational (Desyrel blocks the insomnia sometimes caused by Prozac)—and established by a good deal of clinical research.

Not jumping to the conclusion that the lady in line or the girlfriend or the pharmacist knows more than their doctor helped these patients to address their worries and to be reassured that their doctor knew what he was doing. On the other hand, it's always possible that a doctor has made a mistake. But to assume this and then to act on it—by stopping medication or changing psychiatrists, for example—is a bad idea. Ideally, a psychiatrist can anticipate the sort of worries and challenges his patients may encounter, and prepare them for all the possibilities. But no one can think of all the possibilities, or have the time to discuss them all even if he did.

EPILOGUE

Where does all we've learned leave us? In better relationships, for one thing. Knowing, for example, how psychiatric disorders influence the choice of a partner lets us choose one more wisely. Knowing how the disorders ambush the best of relationships, we can react more judiciously when one emerges and threatens to put us asunder. Knowing that psychiatric disorders keep many of us out of relationships altogether, we can arrange appropriate treatment to get us, or those we care about, past this unhappy exclusion from interpersonal life. Along the way we've learned how biochemical aberrations of brain chemistry underlie all this interpersonal disruption or desolation. Knowing and implementing this makes it much more likely that each of us can enjoy life's deepest pleasures—loving, honoring, and cherishing one another, growing and developing over a lifetime together, and, if we choose, loving and raising children, and cherishing them as they grow to replace us in the order of things.

The protagonist of this book has been the human brain. Nothing we know is more complex or mysterious. Nonetheless, over the last few decades we've begun to explore and exploit (for therapeutic intervention) the details of its myriad centers, pathways, feedback loops, and other systems of checks and balances—all so complex that they still defy description, if not conceptualization. We've found, to put all its one hundred billion neurons in a single phrase, that the brain is much more complex than we ever dreamed, especially when we dreamed with Freud that it was a blank slate onto which early experience inscribed personality.

The mind, on the other hand, seems now much less complex than we once imagined. For example, a person with obsessive-compulsive disorder, we now know, has a deficiency in specific neurotransmitters in specific circuits which suppress other specific circuits. In better times, they work so well that we barely notice them—and in worse, they malfunction and the symptoms of OCD appear. We no longer have to postulate, for example, a convoluted system of regressions and reactivations of Oedipal and pre-Oedipal conflicts, defenses, and deficits that preoccupy or control a person's capacity to think or act. Likewise, we've seen that in the mood disorders, biochemical malfunction brings elements of childlike behavior into adulthood as symptoms of depression or mania. We've seen too that the flight-or-fight reactions of certain people in certain circumstances get out of balance and generate the symptoms of anxiety disorders. The psychological experiences previously understood as the basis for these conditions can now be understood as epiphenomena of the underlying chemical disruption. And so on down the line of the major disorders.

Thus, couples like the Balusteris (of Chapter One) do carry a set of complex psychological baggage from the past, but the engine driving their misery is biochemical derangement. And when the biochemical problems are cleared up with one or another of the psychiatric techniques, much of the distress in each partner, and therefore in their relationship, dissolves away. In most cases there will be a good deal of baggage left over, both from the partners' childhoods and from the effects of years of dealing with the mood disorders and with each other. Often the baggage requires serious attention, including psychotherapy, but as we've seen, psychotherapy works much better after medically based psychiatric treatment sets the brain back to its natural order.

The chances, we've found, that one or both partners in any relationship has one of the seven most common psychiatric disorders that trouble relationships is at least fifty percent—even if we leave aside the minor variants present in almost all of us (and, remember, for reasons of focus and space I've left out alcoholism and other drug abuse). Therefore we must, and fortunately can, treat these disorders, and if we do this in the context of a relationship, the benefits are enhanced manifold.

The time is past for anyone to treat a troubled relationship without considering whether a psychiatric disorder may be initiating the trouble. An internist, for example, treating a woman who complains of fatigue, crying spells, hopelessness, sleeplessness, low energy, and guilt must recognize the depression and arrange for treatment. Likewise, her husband's attorney, in the face of her awkward and halfhearted attempts to divorce her philandering bon vivant of a husband—who's had seven affairs in three weeks, started (and bankrupted) four businesses in two months, barely sleeps, and puns incorrigibly and continuously—must recognize the mania and make the appropriate referral. Failure to recognize these disorders almost certainly will lead to disaster for both partners—probably irreversible disaster—and this is simply not acceptable knowing what medical science has taught us.

Just as important are situations involving more subtle examples of psychiatric disorders—the mild cases of irritability, gloominess, or speediness that don't fit any textbook descriptions but nonetheless damage or terminate countless relationships. If all of us—partners, families, doctors, attorneys, judges, teachers—can learn to identify these minor variants, we can avoid the unnecessary dissolution of many of these relationships. I realize that this is not easy, but since the rewards are tremendous, we need to do our best. Thus, the family doctor of an angry woman who spreads her misery to those closest to her—neglecting and then cuckolding her husband, for example, or verbally abusing and humiliating her children—needs to suspect the unruly sort of depressive we discussed in Chapter Three. A woman like this, you will recall, deals with depression by denying it and passing it on to everyone around her. Or the attorney of her irritable husband (whom she's divorcing because she can't tolerate his angry responses to her infidelity and treatment of their children) needs to consider that the irritability—though it looks like a reasonable response to what his wife is perpetrating on him—may instead be signs of a mild but corrosive angry depression. In the same way, a family court judge needs to recognize conditions like these, and, in his case, order the person in whom he suspects a psychiatric disorder to be evaluated. And on and on through the list of people who try to serve the needs of people in distress. I'm aware that my "musts" and "need-tos" may sound like adolescent idealism, but I doubt they do to anyone who's been through the particular nightmare I've just addressed.

* * *

Throughout this book we've confronted and answered in detail many of the criticisms leveled against psychiatric treatment. We've seen (with Jack and Sonia in Chapter Six, for example) that contrary to what many fear, appropriate psychiatric treatment enhances rather than devalues one's sense of dignity, spirituality, or personal freedom. If anything, recovery from a psychiatric disorder allows a person to have, untarnished and undistorted, his sense of personal dignity, and to hold, without disillusionment or devaluation, whatever set of spiritual convictions move him. The disorders, on the other hand, so cloud a person's ability to use his brain (and therefore his mind) that he loses the full richness of his previous experience of spirituality or dignity.

We've addressed the fear that the doctor and his medications will control his patient, and have shown that on the contrary, the experience of personal freedom becomes much richer with appropriate treatment. Most of the conditions discussed, in fact—especially depression—seriously reduce a person's capacity to make any decision, and therefore the sense of personal freedom becomes much poorer. Treatment doesn't take away any choice, not even that of whether to continue in treatment—even when it's helpful. As we've seen, many people on finding that medication makes them feel better choose to discontinue treatment. They cling to their suffering, immersing themselves in what, to my mind, has become a societywide sickness—the conviction that suffering, especially from a troubled childhood, somehow ennobles a person. They forsake all other agendas, including that of simply feeling better, to seek the heightened sense of personal value they feel only suffering can bring. Fortunately, most people choose to maintain their mental health by cooperating with treatment regimens that work for them.

This book, then, sounds a challenge to everyone—partners and professionals, clients and clinicians—to take the time and to exert the energy to learn about the human brain. This organ, the consummation of a billion years of nature's trials and errors, is a marvelous item, but in any one person, and certainly in any one pair of people, it is very likely to dysfunction in the face of stress. If the dysfunction is troublesome enough, or if it disrupts a relationship badly enough, we must treat it. The first steps to do this are set out in this book—including how to seek out and make the best use of professional help. My intention is to get us past the unnecessary shattering of so many relationships, of so many vows sincerely and fervently made but now fully disavowed—dismembered into regrets, remorse, and memories. Sadly, each memory, each regret, lingers and generates fears and inhibitions that disturb and distort future attempts at relationships—each an epilogue to what could, and should, have been a guide for two people to share each other as long as they live.

It doesn't have to be this way. For a broad sector of trouble in relationships, we now have the capacity to avoid or undo the trouble. That we have the tools to do this is wonderful news, but only if we have the sense and the courage to use them.